POVERTY
The Philippine Scenario

By Ruth S. Callanta

Bookmark

ISBN 971-134-040-2

Printed by S.S.P., Makati, M.M.

Dedication

To all community workers, development managers, and my colleagues in PBSP . . .

because there is so much to do.

because there is so much more that we can share .

ACKNOWLEDGMENT

- Dean Gaby Mendoza of the Asian Institute of Management (AIM) for his guidance and challenge;

- Friends for providing the intellectual stimulation to create the gestalt of this study; in particular, to Vikram, Earl, Didi, Mads, and Ravi;

- Sol and Wency Hernando who, like me, have grappled with the painful question of why, in the midst of bounty, people are poor;

- Paulita Rodriguez for her meticulousness patience in data-gathering;

- Atty. Bienvenido A. Tan, Jr. for showing me the way;

- Ederlina Gamboa and Evelyn Dumlao for helping me beat the deadline;

- Tessa de Chavez for editing this paper;

- Yndiegh L. Felicilda for proofreading;

- PBSP colleagues for the trust, confidence, and much needed support; and

- My family — Ed, Mon and Pan for their understanding.

TABLE OF CONTENTS

FOREWORD

This is an important book.

It is important because it deals with the Philippines' most crucial problem: poverty.

The Philippines has many problems:

• unceasing guerrilla attacks by a growing number of communist insurgents, recurring coup attempts by Marcos loyalists and rebellious elements in the armed forces, a heavily armed and fractious Muslim separatist movement, and ideologically militant, strike-prone leftist labor movement.

• an export labor force, numbering in the hundreds of thousands, battered on and victimized by rapacious recruiters and foreign employers, while an even bigger segment of the population — not only from the poorer but also from the middle classes — dream of migrating to the United States and, failing that, to other developed countries.

• a massive and growing international debt burden that devours a major portion of the country's export earnings.

• a politically unstable government, to name some of the more important ones.

Most, if not all, of these problems, however, have their roots firmly planted in the fact of widespread poverty. A majority of the Filipinos do not earn enough to adequately feed, clothe, and shelter their families. Unless this radical, basic, fundamental problem is solved, there is little hope that long-run and effective solutions will be found for the other major problems of the society.

It is an important book because it collects and makes available for examination and analysis a great deal of scattered information about the situation of the poor in the Philippines.

Many problems in the developing world are intractable not so much because they have no practicable solutions but because the information necessary and relevant to their proper analysis are not collected and, thus, their real causes are never correctly determined. Too often, decisions are made not on the bases of painstaking data gathering and research but on suppositions and assumptions that have only the most tenuous ties to reality.

This examination by Ruth Callanta of the problem of poverty suffers from no such shortcoming. Over a substantial portion of a year, she has put in a lot of work into doing both library and field research. She has meticulously done her homework.

It is an important book because it classifies the major poverty groups, analyzes the causes why each group is poor, and proposes concrete steps that might be taken to eradicate their poverty.

The author has gone about her work professionally. She has not stinted in devoting time to ruffing the evidence that she has collected and compelling them to reveal to her their meaning. Consequently, her facts can face close scrutiny, her analyses can stand criticism, and her conclusions can, unscathed, withstand sharp challenges. She has pushed her thinking, developed her ideas, honed her conclusions and recommendations to the point that they are managerially actionable.

More than four hundred years ago, Francis Bacon wrote, "Some books are to be tasted, others to be swallowed, and some few to be chewed and digested." I suggest that were he alive today, he would have added a fourth category: "some, fewer still, to be acted upon and used to change men's lives." Such as this book on Philippine poverty!

GABINO A. MENDOZA
Don Andres Soriano Distinguished
Professor of Business Management
DECEMBER 31, 1987
PARANAQUE, METRO MANILA

PREFACE

With the force and empathy of poetry, Edwin Markham, in his poem, "The Man With the Hoe," decried the life of the peasant: "the Thing the Lord God made and gave to have dominion over sea and land" but than whom there is no shape more terrible. "A Thing that grieves not and that never hopes," he typifies a "humanity betrayed, plundered, profaned and disinherited.

Even a dispassionate look at poverty in the Philippines reveals that betrayal and disinheritance are, indeed, the lot of the landless agricultural worker and others like him who work close to the soil. They are betrayed because, in a land of promise, they continue to wallow in hardship and hopelessness; disinherited because, in a nation of bounty, they have nothing to own.

So the question may be asked: Why? And what is the extent of this plunder and profanity? Who are those that are "dead to rapture and despair"? Where do they live, and how?

So much has already been done to improve the life of the poor. Government has always considered their concerns a priority. And as a result of the rise of non-government voluntary organizations, more programs have been set up to meet the problem.

Yet, despite all these efforts, common observation can only lead to the conclusion that, instead of diminishing, the situation continues to progressively deteriorate. Resources are available; and, by and large, the efforts to bring them to where they belong seem sincere. But the problem persists. Could it be that the cause of the problem has not been accurately diagnosed? Could it be that philosophies and ideologies have gotten in the way? Or that the tools of analysis have been inadequate? In other words, has the poverty problem been sufficiently and objectively analyzed?

It is the search for answers to these questions — and for solutions to problems they pose — that this study was undertaken. This book, therefore, is an attempt at a phenomenology of Philippine poverty. It proceeds from the premise that effective assistance to the poor can be developed only if the situation is accepted, free from *a priori* value judgments. It attempts to look at poverty as a phenomenon that lives and grows upon itself, rather than as a problem resulting from faulty socio-political structures and ideological frameworks. Who are the poor, and why? How do they regard themselves and their needs? And based on their own pragmatic concerns, what should they do and have?

This book has been prepared to provide a picture of the poverty situation in the Philippines. It is offered to planners/decision-makers of poverty alleviation programs — and all those concerned about doing something with, and for, the poor. Hopefully, its findings can serve as a takeoff point in the development of more responsive programs for Philippine society's 70% marginalized and dispossessed who — if their needs continue to be unmet — cry, again to quote Markham, "protest to the Powers of the world, a protest that is also a prophecy."

RUTH S. CALLANTA

IF THE LAND COULD SPEAK,
IT WOULD SPEAK FOR US.
IT WOULD SAY, LIKE US, THAT THE YEARS
HAVE FORGED THE BOND OF LIFE THAT TIES US
    TOGETHER.
IT WAS OUR LABOR THAT MADE THE LAND SHE IS;
AND IT WAS HER YIELDING THAT GAVE US LIFE.
WE AND THE LAND ARE ONE!

BUT WHO WOULD LISTEN?
WILL THEY LISTEN,
THOSE INVISIBLE,
WHO, FROM AN UNFEELING DISTANCE, CLAIM
THE LAND IS THEIRS?
BECAUSE PIECES OF PAPER SAY SO?
BECAUSE THE PIECES OF PAPER ARE BACKED BY MEN
WHO SPEAK THREATENING WORDS.
MEN WHO HAVE POWER TO SHOOT AND TO KILL,
MEN WHO HAVE POWER TO TAKE OUR MEN AND OUR
    SONS AWAY?

IF THE LAND COULD SPEAK
IT WOULD SPEAK FOR US!
FOR THE LAND IS US!

Translated From A Poem By:
Macli-ing Dulag

CHAPTER I
THE POVERTY SCENARIO

CONCEPTS AND MEASUREMENTS OF POVERTY

Definition of Poverty

The study of poverty appears to be highly subjective, directed as much by the value judgments of the researcher as by the statistics he gathers.

While there have been numerous definitions and measurements advanced (Appendix A), the basic argument appears to be that the poor are those whose incomes *barely maintain their physical existence* and *those who have limited* or *no means of access to other social needs.*

At present, three concepts of poverty are being used in the Philippines: relative poverty, absolute poverty, and poverty according to the perception of the people themselves.

Poverty can be understood in terms of the relative share in income or consumption of various sectors, such as the income share accruing to the lowest 20% or 40% of the population. The National Economic and Development Authority (NEDA) and the National Census and Statistics Office (NCSO) define the low-income group as those households/families belonging to the bottom 30% of the income bracket. The World Bank (WB), on the other hand, suggests a per capita income level equivalent to the lower 45 percentile for all developing countries (WB 1980). Most countries use the bottom 40% of the total income bracket.

Absolute poverty can be measured in terms of the capacity of a group to meet specified minimum needs (poverty line). This does not imply that all persons falling below the poverty line are either equally or absolutely deprived. Among the absolute poor, those near the top of the group may only be on the margin of subsistence whereas those at the bottom may be seriously deprived.

Measurement of absolute poverty incidence offers a great deal of arbitrariness and uncertainty. For instance, poverty incidence for the Philippines as estimated by various researchers ranges between 45% and 64.3% of all total households. This difference stems from: (a) the need to draw a poverty line based on some idea of minimum needs to be able to identify the poor; (b) varying needs of individuals; (c) different conditions obtaining in the different areas of the country; (d) significant variances in consumption requirements and prices of goods and services; and (e) the income and expenditure data, as collected, may be affected by temporary factors, i.e , effects of natural calamities and poor harvest, among others.

Another measure to determine poverty incidence is advanced by Mangahas (1977). To arrive at a threshold, poverty is measured through the use of perception variables (e.g.,perceived minimum needs in order that a family can consider itself non-poor). Mangahas argues that since a poverty line is a normative concept (i.e., is related to human values), every Filipino can set his own standard for it. Thus, respondents are generally asked what they would consider to be the minimum income level to be able to maintain a standard of living considered to be non-poor.

The Poverty Line

The two main instruments used for drawing a poverty line to measure absolute poverty are the consumption basket of the "representative poor" and the least-cost consumption basket necessary to meet specified minimum needs. In each case, the major component of the consumption basket is food.

The representative consumption basket has the advantage of using the actual consumption pattern of the poor, presumably reflecting their preferences. Among the studies which have used this method was the National Food and Agriculture Survey conducted in November 1970.

The least-cost consumption basket approach, on the other hand, attempts to meet the minimum recommended dietary and other subsistence requirements at the lowest possible cost. Its advantage is that it determines the income necessary to meet the minimum needs of an individual (or a family). If the individual then chooses to spend the income on unnecessary items or on food that is not cost-efficient (i.e., provides less nutrition per peso spent), this decision reflects his preferences, not food deprivation.

In 1980, the World Bank calculated the Philippine poverty line based on the 1970 actual consumption estimates of the National Food and Agriculture Council (NFAC), and the least-cost figure estimated by Tan and Holazo (1979). The World Bank arrived at a poverty line of ₱500 per capita per year for 1971. This was ten percent below the actual preference consumption basket but 40% above the least-cost consumption basket.

Between 1974-75, Ma. Alcestis S. Abrera undertook one of the more thorough analyses of absolute poverty thresholds in the Philippines. She adopted a basic menu designed and recommended by the Food and Nutrition Research Center to promote a nutritionally adequate minimum cost diet which was determined to cost a reference family of six in Manila ₱18 per day in May 1974.

Utilizing food price indices to translate this figure into prices of other years and regional urban and rural cost of living deflators to adjust for geographic variations in such prices, Abrera constructed an array of food poverty threshold figures for different years and different locations. She also utilized per capita estimates to calculate specific food threshold by area and family size. Any household whose total annual income is less than that required to feed itself is considered absolutely poor.

Table 1 provides the relevant thresholds for a household of six for different years according to place of residence.

With reference to the poverty line as perceived by the people themselves, a nationwide socio-political opinion survey conducted by the Bishops-Businessmen's Conference in 1985 revealed that the perceived median poverty line for the whole Philippines is ₱1,500 per month or ₱18,000 per year. For Metro Manila, the median poverty line is ₱3,000 (₱36,000 per

5

year). Elsewhere in the country, the most common figure given is ₱1,500, although this is as low as ₱1,000 in rural Luzon and as high as ₱1,700 in urban Visayas. The same survey revealed that by their own perceptions, 74% of Filipinos regard themselves as poor, and another 13% regard themselves as on the borderline of poverty.

Table 1. Poverty Lines for Household of Six (in Pesos).

YEAR	Rural	Urban	Manila	PHILIPPINES
1971	3,000	3,428	4,284	3,570
1975	5,201	5,943	7,123	6,089

Source: Abrera, Ma. Alcestis "Philippine Poverty Thresholds" in Mahar Mangahas, ed. *Measuring Philippine Development*. Development Academy of the Philippines. 1976.

Sensitivity and Calculation of Poverty Incidence

Since poverty line is an approximation, poverty incidence is sensitive to changes in the poverty line. Table 2 shows the variances in poverty levels in the Philippines based on the different poverty line estimates of various researchers.

Poverty incidence could be calculated for either individuals or families. However, from a strategy/policy point of view, it is more appropriate to construct the poverty profile in terms of family characteristics and the family head because this approach also captures the dependents of the income earner. Hence, poverty incidences by family are given in this study.

THE EXTENT, PATTERN AND TRENDS OF POVERTY

Extent of Poverty Incidence in the Philippines

Using the poverty line estimates advanced by various researchers, poverty incidence in the Philippines in 1971 was anywhere between 30% to 56% of total families. This means 1.89 million to 3.53 million families who can barely maintain their physical existence and who have limited or no means of access to other social needs.

In 1975, the percent of total families below the poverty line increased from 30% to 64.3% of all Filipino families. In absolute figures, this means at least 2.10 to 4.51 million families in relative or absolute poverty.

Assuming that the same proportion of poor families exist for 1985, the total families below the poverty line at the current population of 54.49 million, would be from 2.72 to 5.84 million. This figure will increase to 6.72 million. Computations are based on the results of the BBC survey where 74% of Filipinos consider themselves poor (Table 2).

Characteristics/Composition of Poverty Incidence

Poverty Incidence by Location

From Abrera's analysis, 56% of all Filipino families reported incomes below the food threshold in 1971. The incidence of poverty by family was 64% in rural areas, 34% in Manila and 39% in other urban areas. Taking the families below the threshold as a group to determine its composition, 78.2% were in rural areas, 5.4% in Manila and 15.8% in other urban areas.

Converting the number of families into population figures, 60.5% of all people were below the poverty line. The corresponding incidence of poverty figures by population area showed

7

Table 2. Extent of Poverty Incidence in the Philippines, 1971, 1975, 1985.

RESEARCHER/ YEAR	1971			1975			1985		
	Poverty Line ₱	% of Families Below Poverty Line	Absolute[1] No. of Families (000)	Poverty Line ₱	% of Families Below Poverty Line	Absolute[2] No. of Families (000)	Poverty Line ₱	% of Families Below Poverty Line	Absolute[3] No. of Families (000)
NEDA/ NCSO	bottom 30%	30.0	1,889	bottom 30%	30.0	2,103	bottom 30%	30.0	2,724
Tan	2,160	42.09	2,645	3,572	45.08	3,155	10,305	45.18	4,094
World Bank	3,000	38.7	2,437	4,962	45.3	3,176	14,315	45.3	4,114
Abrera	3 570	56.0	3,527	6,089	64.3	4,509	17,567	64.3	5,840
BBC/ Mangahas	–	–	–	–	–	–	18,000	74.0	6,720

[1] Philippine population at 37,785,020 or 6,297,503 families.

[2] Philippine population at 42,070,660 or 7,011,776 families

[3] Philippine population at 54,488,000 or 9,081,000 families.

Sources: Tan; E.A. and V. Holazo. "Measuring Poverty Incidence in a Segmental Market: The Philippine Cases." The Philippine Economic Journal. XVIII.

Abrera, Ma. Alcestis. "Philippine Poverty Thresholds" in Mahar Mangahas ed. *Measuring Philippine Development*. Development Academy of the Philippines, 1976.

Philippine Statistical Yearbook 1984, National Economic and Development Authority.

that 68.9% would be in the rural areas, 39% in Manila, and 43.6% in other urban areas (Table 3).

Table 3. Poverty Incidence by Urban and Rural Classification, 1971

	PHILIPPINES	Manila & Suburbs	Other Urban	Rural
% families below the food threshold	56.0	34.0	39.0	64.0
% distribution of all poor families	100.0	5.4	15.8	78.2
% distribution of total poor people	60.5	39.1	43.6	68.9

Source: Abrera, Ma. Alcestis. "Philippine Poverty Thresholds" in Mahar Mangahas ed. *Measuring Philippine Development*. Development Academy of the Philippines, 1976.

With reference to the incidence and composition of poverty by region (Table 4), the highest percentage of families below the food threshold was in East Visayas (11.77%), South Mindanao (7.75%) and Central Luzon (6.98%).

Poverty incidence increased substantially in 1975 from its 1971 levels.

The World Bank calculated that the poverty incidence for the whole country was 45% compared to 38.7% in 1971. Abrera noted that 64.3% of the total population was below the food threshold.

The highest percentage increase in poverty incidence between 1971 and 1975 was in Metro Manila, Central Luzon, Northern Mindanao and Southern Mindanao (Table 5).

Using Abrera's analysis, poverty incidence in 1975 did not vary substantially across regions. The regions with the highest poverty incidence were Western Mindanao, Northern Mindanao, Eastern Visayas and Bicol. The highest concentrations of the poor were in the most populous regions of Southern Tagalog, Western Visayas and Metro Manila (Table 6).

9

Table 4. Incidence and Composition of Poverty by Region, Philippines, 1971.

REGION	Total No. of Families	% Distribution of Total	No. of Families Below Threshold	No. of Families Below Threshold	% of Total Poor Families
PHILIPPINES	6,347	100.0	60.9	3,866	100.0
Manila and Suburbs	525	8.27	3.37	214	5.5
Ilocos, Mt. Province	346	5.45	3.69	234	6.0
Cagayan, Batanes	260	4.09	3.29	209	5.4
Central Luzon	855	13.47	6.98	443	11.5
South Tagalog	869	13.69	6.95	441	11.4
Bicol	496	7.81	5.31	337	8.7
West Visayas	670	10.55	6.87	436	11.3
East Visayas	980	15.44	11.77	747	19.3
North Mindanao	522	8.22	4.91	312	8.1
South Mindanao	825	12.99	7.75	492	12.7

Sources: Calculated from *"Family Income and Expenditures."* 1975. Special Release No. 190. NCSO, March 1977.
Abrera, Ma. Alcestis "Philippine Poverty Thresholds" in Mahar Mangahas, ed. *Measuring Philippine Development.* Development Academy of the Philippines. 1976.

With reference to 1985, the only available study that would give an indication of poverty incidence by location was the survey done by the Bishops-Businessmen's Conference. Of the 74% Filipinos who considered themselves poor, 88% came from the rural areas. In Metro Manila, 50% of the people regarded themselves as poor; in other urban areas, it ranged from 60% to 77%.

Table 5. Regional Poverty Incidence in the Philippines Based on Levels Used by Various Researchers for 1971 and 1975.

REGIONS	1971		1975		
	Tan	WB	Tan	WB	Abrera
Metro Manila	13.63	9.1	35.82	30.9	57.6
Ilocos I	56.11	41.7	43.46	38.5	64.5
Cagayan Valley	65.32	54.7	52.66	45.7	66.6
Central Luzon	30.07	17.6	27.47	28.9	61.0
S. Tagalog	49.12	35.1	39.42	45.9	65.2
Bicol	49.12	48.8	55.07	55.4	71.1
W. Visayas	36.05	38.3	49.07	48.0	65.0
C. Visayas[1]	—	64.7	—	59.9	56.5
E. Visayas	60.05	59.7	47.99	56.0	73.0
W. Mindanao[2]	45.40	38.1	63.38	45.9	73.9
N. Mindanao	—	58.2	—	72.8	72.5
S. Mindanao	42.09	39.7	49.48	41.5	61.8
Central Mindanao	—	20.4	—	31.7	60.2
ALL REGIONS	42.09	38.7	45.08	48.3	64.3

[1] Used to be part of E. Visayas
[2] Used to be part of S. Mindanao
Sources: Tan, Holazo, Abrera, Ma. Alcestis, NCSO, 1975.

Poverty Incidence by Size of Family

In studies conducted by Valerio et. al. (1984) and the World Bank (1980), it appeared that the larger the family, the higher the incidence of poverty. The World Bank estimated that families with six or more members constituted about 52% of total families in the Philippines.

On the other hand, Valerio et. al. found out that more than half of the impoverished groups had more than six household members (52.6%) which was higher than the average household size of six. There were 26.3% of the poor households who had 5-6 household members, 17.1% with 3-4 members, and 4.0% with 1-2 members (Table 7).

11

Table 6. Incidence and Composition of Poverty by Region, Philippines 1975.

REGION	Total No. of Families	% Distribution of Total	% of Families Below Threshold	No. of Families Below Threshold	% of Total Families
PHILIPPINES	6,859	100.0	64.3	4,413	100.0
Metro Manila	770	11.2	57.6	444	10.1
Ilocos	558	8.1	64.5	360	8.2
Cagayan Valley	329	4.8	66.6	219	5.0
Central Luzon	662	9.7	61.0	404	9.1
S. Tagalog	888	12.9	64.2	570	12.9
Bigol	518	7.6	71.1	368	8.3
W. Visayas	679	9.9	65.0	441	10.0
C. Visayas[1]	595	8.7	56.5	336	7.6
E. Visayas	441	6.4	73.0	332	7.3
W. Mindanao[2]	314	4.6	73.9	232	5.3
N. Mindanao	370	5.4	72.5	268	6.1
S. Mindanao	433	6.3	61.8	268	6.1
C. Mindanao[3]	301	4.4	60.2	181	4.1

[1]Used to be part of E. Visayas,

[2]Used to be part of S. Mindanao

[3]Some provinces used to be part of N. Mindanao and some from S. Mindanao.

Sources: Calculated from *"Family Income and Expenditures."* 1975. Special Release No. 190, NCSO, March 1977.
Food Poverty Threshold adapted from Abrera, Ma. Alcestis "Philippine Poverty Thresholds" in Mahar Mangahas, ed. *Measuring Philippine Development*. Development Academy of the Philippines. 1976.

Table 7. Percentage Distribution of Households Below Food Threshold by Household Size, Philippines, 1978.

HOUSEHOLD SIZE	Percent of Total Households Below Food Threshold
1 – 2	4.0
3 – 4	17.1
5 – 6	26.3
7 and above	52.6
TOTAL	100.0

Source: Valerio, Teresita E., Domdom, A. and Villavieja, G., "An Analysis of Food Threshold in the Philippines," FNRI-NSTA. 1983.

NSTA. 1983.

These results lend support to the hypothesis that low-income families tend to be large and large families tend to be poor because of their high dependency ratios and lower capacity for saving and investment. This suggests that poverty redressal would simultaneously require family planning, more employment opportunities and decreased dependency in larger families.

Poverty Incidence by Occupation [1]

The highest 1971 incidence rates of poverty were found in the household head occupational categories of "farmers, farm laborers, fishermen, hunters, loggers, and related workers" (75%), "manual workers and laborers not elsewhere classified" (70%), "craftsmen and production process workers" and the "unemployed without work experience and those household heads not in the labor force" (71%) (Table 8).

---

[1] There is no separate data available from the 1975 FIES. Hence, the discussion is limited to 1971.

Table 8. Indicence of poverty by Major Occupational Group of Household Head, Urban and Rural, Philippines, 1971.

MAJOR OCCUPATIONAL GROUP OF HOUSEHOLD HEAD	Percentage Incidence of Poverty [1]			
	PHILIPPINES	Manila & Suburbs	Other Urban	Rural
Professional, technical and related workers	11.6	4.4	14.7	12.5
Admin., executive and managerial	14.0	2.7	16.8	16.7
Clerical	22.3	24.2	23.5	18.9
Sales	45.7	37.7	38.6	56.8
Farmers, farm laborers, fishermen, hunters, loggers and related workers	75.4	—	62.2	76.4
Miners, quarrymen and related	—	—	—	—
Transportation and communication	50.4	56.6	49.8	48.4
Craftsmen, production process workers	59.3	59.7	55.8	61.8
Manual workers and laborers not elsewhere classified	69.9	77.5	79.0	63.3
Service, sports and related workers	48.0	46.7	50.3	46.7
Unemployed without work experience and those not in labor force	60.3	28.8	51.2	70.6
Occupation not reported	—	—	—	—
TOTAL	62.0	40.7	46.7	69.3

[1] Percentage of families with income below 1971 Food Threshold as defined by Ma. Alcestis S. Abrera, "Philippine Poverty Thresholds," in Mahar Mangahas, ed. *Measuring Philippine Development*. Development Academy of the Philippines. 1976, pp. 236-241. The food threshold values estimated for 1971 were P4,284 for Greater Manila, P3,428 for other urban areas, and P3,000 for rural areas. At P6.44/$, these values $665, $532 and $466, respectively, per household, or $111, $89 and $78, respectively, per capita in 1971 dollars.

Source: Calculated from *"Family Income and Expenditures."* 1971. The BCS Survey of Households Bulletin. Bureau fo Census and Statistics. Manila.

Poverty Incidence by Main Source of Family Income

Classified by main source of family income, the highest poverty incidence rates were found among those families relying mainly on farming (79%), fishing, forestry and hunting (77%), and wages and salaries (71%). Those engaged in rural manufacturing and trading activities also suffered high rates of poverty incidence (72% and 76%, respectively) (Table 9).

Table 9. Composition of Poverty by Main Source of Family Income Urban and Rural 1971.

Main Source of Income	NO. OF FAMILIES BELOW FOOD THRESHOLD[1] (1000)				PERCENTAGE OF PHILIPPINE TOTAL			
	Philip-pines	Manila & Suburbs	Other Urban	Rural	Philip-pines	Manila & Suburbs	Other Urban	Rural
Wages and Salaries	1,321.2	162.5	359.4	799.3	33.6	4.1	9.1	20.3
Agricultural	484.5	0.4	32.9	451.2	12.3	0.01	0.8	11.5
Non-agricultural	836.2	162.1	326.3	347.8	21.3	4.1	8.3	8.8
Entrepreneurial Activities	2,366.9	26.3	228.1	2,112.5	60.2	0.7	5.8	53.7
Trading	208.9	14.5	75.9	118.5	5.3	0.4	1.9	3.0
Manufacturing	128.9	5.7	36.8	86.4	3.3	0.14	0.9	2.2
Transport	39.8	0.9	10.4	28.5	1.0	0.02	0.3	0.7
Other Enterprises	35.9	2.8	16.4	16.7	0.9	0.07	0.04	0.4
Profession or Trade	11.4	2.6	4.5	4.3	0.3	0.07	0.1	0.1
Farming (including livestock and poultry)	1,731.9	—	60.9	1,671.0	44.1	—	1.5	42.5
Fishing, Forestry and Hunting	209.7	—	23.2	186.5	5.3	—	0.6	4.7
Other Sources	228.4	9.5	59.2	159.7	5.8	0.2	1.5	4.1
Source not identified in data	15.0	15.0			0.4	0.4		
TOTAL	3,931.4	213.2	646.7	3,071.5	100.0	5.4	16.4	78.1

[1] Number of families with incomes below 1971 Food Threshold as defined by Ma. Alcestis S. Abrera, Philippine Poverty Thresholds", in Mahar Mangahas, ed., *Measuring Philippine Development,* The Development Academy of the Philippines, 1976, pp. 236-41. The food threshold values estimated for 1971 were ₱4,284 for Greater Manila, ₱3,428 for other urban areas, and ₱3,000 for rural areas, at ₱6.44/$, these values equal $665, $532 and $466, respectively, per household, or $111, $89 and $78, respectively, per capita, in 1971 dollars.

Source: Calculated from Family Income and Expenditures: 1971, the BCS Survey of Households Bulletin.

Poverty Incidence by Sector/Sub-Sector

By sub-sector, about 70% of the poor families in agriculture nationwide and a majority of all regions were dependent on rice and corn farming. Rice and corn together accounted for about 60%, of the value of agricultural production, 50-60%, of area, and about 71% of employment (World Bank 1980). The remainder of the poor families in the agricultural sector were in fishing, hunting and trapping (10.4%), coconut farming (9.3%), other crops farming (5.9%), and sugar cane farming (3.7%).

The major agricultural occupations and sub-sectors showed relatively small variation in poverty incidence. By occupation, farmer-tenants and farmers unclassified by tenancy showed the highest poverty incidence (59% and 57%, respectively) and full owners (48%). The apparent low variation in poverty incidence among the major occupations and sub-sectors reflected some important characteristics of Philippine agriculture: (a) the predominance of small farm size and pervasiveness of tenancy in various crops; (b) the existence of multiple sources of family income, including non-farm employment (and remittances from urban areas); and (c) the difficulty of classifying different types of farming since many farmers have 2-3 parcels of land, each with different cropping patterns and tenancy arrangements.

Income Distribution and Poverty Incidence (1975)

Table 10 shows the average 1975 annual income of families belonging to the bottom 40% of the population, grouped by decile. The lowest tenth of families in the country had an average annual income of ₱1,425 while the fourth tenth of families had an average annual income of ₱3,507. The table also shows that Regions X (N. Mindanao), VIII (E. Visayas), V (Bicol), II (Cagayan Valley) and IX (Western Mindanao) had the lowest average incomes among the bottom 40% of the population.

16

Table 10. Average Income of Families by Tenths of Families by Region, Philippines, 1975 (Preliminary data based on the results on hand tally).

RANKING OF FAMILIES (LOWEST TO HIGHEST INCOME)	First Tenth	Second Tenth	Third Tenth	Fourth Tenth
PHILIPPINES	1,425	2,341	2,932	3,507
M.M/NCR	2,376	3,343	4,026	4,840
Region I	1,563	2,514	3,187	3,696
II	1,277	2,209	2,645	3,158
III	1,753	2,704	3,254	3,887
IV	1,331	2,279	2,904	3,525
V	1,196	1,890	2,355	2,846
VI	1,586	2,401	2,886	3,328
VII	1,068	2,065	2,659	3,224
VIII	1,303	1,931	2,409	2,875
IX	1,268	1,805	2,507	2,989
X	833	1,678	2,164	2,554
XI	1,571	2,386	2,986	3,573
XII	1,673	2,252	2,822	3,596

Source: *Philippine Statistical Yearbook 1984,* National Economic and Development Authority.

The largest concentration of families having incomes below ₱4,999 or within the bottom 40% is in N. Mindanao (Region X), Bicol (Region V) and Western Mindanao (Region IX) (Table 11).

Table 11. Distribution of Families by Income Class and Region, Philippines, 1975.

REGION/ YEAR	NO. OF FAMILIES (000)	PERCENTAGE DISTRIBUTION BY INCOME						
		ALL INCOME GROUPS	UNDER ₱1000	₱1000 to ₱1,999	₱2,000 to ₱2,999	₱3,000 to ₱3,999	₱4,000 to ₱4,999	TOTAL
PHILIPPINES	6,859	100.0	2.7	11.0	18.6	17.4	13.2	62.9
MM Area/ NCR	770	100.0	0.2	1.2	11.3	14.5	14.5	41.7
Region I: Ilocos Region	558	100.0	1.2	10.3	15.5	20.0	16.5	63.5
Region II: Cagayan Valley	329	100.0	3.1	9.7	24.1	16.0	10.6	63.5
Region III: Central Luzon	662	100.0	2.6	6.3	16.4	18.2	13.1	56.6
Region IV: Southern Tagalog	886	100.0	2.1	6.4	15.2	16.1	13.1	52.9
Region V: Bicol Region	518	100.0	3.1	18.6	21.9	18.1	13.5	75.2
Region VI: Western Visayas	679	100.0	5.8	10.1	17.5	17.8	14.7	65.4
Region VII: Central Visayas	595	100.0	5.8	10.1	17.5	17.8	14.7	65.9
Region VIII: Eastern Visayas	441	100.0	1.4	15.2	22.6	7.9	13.0	60.1
Region IX: Western Mindanao	314	100.0	—	22.4	21.4	18.6	10.1	72.5
Region X Northern Mindanao	433	100.0	12.9	20.9	21.0	13.8	8.9	77.5
Region XI: Southern Mindanao	370	100.0	0.3	10.5	16.2	18.2	14.9	60.1
Region XII: Central Mindanao	301	100.0	0.1	9.5	25.0	14.0	14.6	63.2

Source: *Philippine Statistical Yearbook 1984*, National Economic and Development Authority, p. 12.

Poverty Trends — 1955-1975

A number of income distribution and expenditure surveys have been conducted in the Philippines[2], of which at least five major expenditure surveys have been published including several quarterly surveys for much smaller sampling frames between 1978 and 1980. An analysis of the results of these surveys was

---

[2] Six major expenditure surveys have been conducted: 1956, 1961, 1965, 1971, 1975, and 1980. However, results of the 1981 survey have not been published.

done by J.M. Dowling, Jr. and D. Soo in their study "Income Distribution and Economic Growth" published by the Asian Development Bank. The authors concluded that very little progress, if any, has been made in improving income distribution in the past twenty years in the Philippines. This conclusion is supported by the following findings:

1. Both the results of the major expenditure surveys and the small surveys conducted between 1978-81 showed uniformly high Gini-coefficients reflecting the poor distribution of income which has prevailed in the Philippines for a long time. Despite moderate land reform in recent years the distribution still tended to be very unequal (Table 12).

Table 12. Gini-coefficients for the Philippines, 1956-1981

YEAR	GINI-COEFFICIENTS
1956	.4540
1961	.4644
1965	.4632
1971	.4536
1975	.4220
1978 (II)	.4700
1978 (III)	.4920
1979 (I)	.4952
1979 (II)	.4816
1979 (III)	.4954
1979 (IV)	.4783
1980 (III)	.5033
1980 (IV)	.4653
1981 (III)	.5032

Source: J.M. Dowling and D. Soo. "Income Distribution and Economic Growth." Staff Paper No.15. Asian Development Bank.

2. Income inequality had deteriorated since 1961. The share of the lowest quantile had declined from about five percent to less than three percent, while that of the top 20 percent had increased to nearly 60 percent (Table 13).

Table 13. Quantile Share of Low and High Income Earners, Philippines, 1956-1981.

YEAR	Share of Bottom of 20 percent	Share of top 20 percent	Ratio 2/1
	(1)	(2)	
1956	4.9	54.8	11.2
1961	4.2	56.2	13.4
1965	3.6	55.4	15.4
1971	3.9	54.0	13.8
1975	5.5	53.3	9.7
1978 (II)	3.4	56.0	16.5
1978 (III)	3.2	58.2	18.2
1979 (I)	3.1	58.9	19.0
1979 (II)	3.1	56.8	18.3
1979 (III)	3.2	58.9	18.4
1979 (IV)	3.6	57.0	15.8
1980 (III)	2.8	59.4	21.2
1980 (IV)	3.2	54.7	17.1
1981 (III)	2.8	59.4	21.1

Source: Dowling and Soo.

With reference to the pattern of regional poverty incidence, estimates by various researchers consistently placed Northern Mindanao, Eastern and Western Visayas, Bicol and the Cagayan Valley as the areas having the highest incidence of poverty. In addition, there had been rapid increase in poverty incidence between 1971 to 1975 in Metro Manila, Central Luzon, Central Mindanao and Southern Tagalog.

3. Deteriorating Regional Income Distribution

Evidence of deteriorating income distribution by region was also present in the results of the major household expenditure surveys. Comparing Gini ratios from the beginning and ending period for 1978 and 1981, a tendency towards low and deteriorating income distribution had been observed. All but two of the regions had larger Gini-coefficients in the latter period. The average Gini-coefficient for all regions also increased. Aside from 1985, all the income distribution studies point to high and increasing income inequality.

In addition to the above study done by Dowling and Soo showing the relative position of the poor vis-a-vis the total population, absolute poverty trends can also be deduced using the poverty line estimates. Three studies have been previously cited: those by Tan and Holazo, the World Bank, and Ma. Alcestis Abrera. While poverty incidence was reduced between 1957 and 1965 without exception, the results suggest that there had been a significant trend towards increased poverty since then (Table 14).

Table 14. Estimatte of the Proportions in Poverty, 1965-1975.

YEAR	Tan & Holazo	WB1*	WB2*	Abrera
1957			72.1	
1961			57.9	
1965	36.71	37.2	43.3	
1971	42.09	38.7	44.9	56.0
1975	45.8	45.3	53.2	64.3

*WB1 measured poverty in per capita income, while WB2 measured porverty in terms of family/household income.

POVERTY INCIDENCE AND ACCESS
TO BASIC SOCIAL SERVICES

Lamberte (1983) defined access as "the relationship between the administrative allocation of resources and the target groups of people who need them and for whom they are intended. Operationally, access is measured in terms of the allocation of resources to specified target groups. The degree of access is seen in the number of people who directly benefit from the sources of assistance, the amount of specific services extended to the area itself, or both (Ibid.).

Lamberte, in her study, asserted that there are serious imbalances in the delivery of basic social services in the Philippines. This imbalance is due to: (a) unequal investment in public services within jurisdiction and among regions (WB 1980)[3]; (b) the priority given by regional development thrusts towards the National Capital Region, Central Luzon and Southern Tagalog (Pernia and others 1981); and (c) lack of government intervention in the provision of services.

Lamberte, based on an analysis of data gathered, concluded that the level of development of the provinces is directly related to the level of access to services. Most of the provinces having least access to services — particularly agricultural services, health, education, and physical infrastructure — corresponded closely with identified less-developed areas. Of these, the most disadvantaged groups belonged to the uplands.

The following discussion focuses on the access of the population to basic goods and services, e.g., food and nutrition, health, education, housing, water supply and sewerage. Indicators such as incidence of malnutrition, life expectancy and morbidity reflect the impact of the levels of both private incomes and public services. They also capture the degree of satisfaction of the beneficiary groups. Likewise, they serve to cross-check

---

[3]This includes public utilities such as water supply and sewerage, health and education facilities, transport and financial institutions.

22

the expenditures/income-based profile. The available information can, thus, indicate the areas, groups or sectors which need special attention.

Food and Nutrition

The First Nationwide Nutrition Survey (FNNS) showed that, in 1978, calorie consumption in the Philippines averaged 89% of the Recommended Daily Allowance (RDA).

Variations were noted in nutritional adequacy across geographical areas. Rural areas had a lower adequacy level than urban areas. Similarly, Visayas and Mindanao island groups were a little worse off than Luzon. Shortage of food, inadequate and unbalanced food intake, poor consumption habits, low or unequal incomes, or any combination of these factors may be responsible for malnutrition.

The NEDA Statistical Coordination Office, in a 1975 study, stated that the country's food supply over the years was adequate to meet the population's overall requirements for calories and protein. Yet in 1978, nutritional intake, except for protein, was inadequate. The explanation for this seeming contradiction obviously stemmed from the fact that nearly 60% of the people had inadequate incomes to purchase and consume nutritionally sufficient quantities of food.

RDA per person for the Philippines as a whole, as given in FNNS, was: calorie = 2,036; protein = 51.5 gm; iron = 12.0 ug; Vitamin A = 3,618 I.U. The RDAs for the urban and rural areas and for various island groups were marginally different.

Moreover, the Philippines is the 14th largest food producer, 80 percent of Filipino children are malnourished. An MOH-FNRI survey in 1982 disclosed that seven out of ten schoolchildren suffered from some form of malnutrition.

According to the 1982 FNRI national survey, Filipinos were, on the average, lacking in all but one nutrient, niacin. Daily per capita intake of other nutrients fell below prescribed adequate levels. The protein adequacy level of 102.9 percent in

1978 fell to 99.6 percent in 1982. Iron adequacy level likewise went down from 91.7 percent to 91.5 percent during the same period.

As of February 1985, FNRI calculated that the daily food requirements of a family of six cost about ₱64.70 compared with an effective minimum wage of ₱57.08 a day.

Table 15 shows a conservative estimate of the number of Filipinos who have been consuming marginally for the past three years.

Table 15. Proportion of Households that do not Meet the Adequate Food Requirements, 1982-1984.

INDICATORS	PHILIPPINES	METRO MANILA
Third Quarter 1982		
Minimum adequate food expenditure	₱1,620.00	
Proportion of households that do not get adequate food needs	31.5%	6.2%
Third Quarter 1983		
Minimum adequate food expenditures	₱1,809.00	
Proportion of households that do not get adequate food needs	35.1%	6.1%
Second Quarter 1984		
Minimum adequate food expenditure	₱2,700.00	
Proportion of households that do not get adequate food needs	n.a.	17.8%

NOTES:

1. 1983 and 1984 minimum food budget estimated based on 1982-1983 inflation rate for food — 11 and 49 percent, respectively. (NEDA, National Income Accounts CY 1982-1984, advance estimates as of December 1984).

2. Each household assumed to be composed of an average of six members in the family.

Health

The generally accepted indicators of the health status of a population are life expectancy, mortality and morbidity. Key sectoral indicators manifested improved health and nutrition performance in 1983. The average life expectancy was estimated to have increased to 62.5 years in 1983, higher by 0.3 years than the 1982 estimate. The crude death rate was calculated to have decreased to 8.2 deaths per 1,000 population while the infant mortality rate was estimated to have declined to 59 deaths per 1,000 live births. The prevalence of children below 75 percent of standard weight declined to 17.57 percent among preschoolers and 22.86 percent among schoolchildren. Meanwhile, the Medicare Program expanded its coverage to 22.8 million individuals, benefitting some 1.5 million members during the year (NEDA 1984).

The leading causes of morbidity in 1979 were influenza, digestive diseases (gastroenteritis, colitis and dysentery), bronchitis, tuberculosis, and pneumonia.

NEDA surmised that although there had been a continuing decline in crude birth rate, infant and child mortality rate levels still remained high. The total number of birth per thousand population is estimated at 32.5 in 1974 or 0.4 percentage points lower than that in 1983. The infant mortality rate per thousand live births was estimated to have declined 1.3 percentage points in 1984 while the crude death rate per thousand population was estimated to be slightly lower during the year. Average life expectancy improved by 0.5 percent to 62.8 years in 1984 (NEDA).

A staggering disparity existed between NEDA and IBON reports on the number of medical personnel available. IBON estimated that for every 20,000 population in the countryside, there was only one health personnel available (*Bulletin Today,* 4 July 1983). NEDA, on the other hand, scaled down the figure to a very much lower ratio of one physician to 2,661 persons, one nurse to 2,950 persons and one midwife to 3,087 persons.

25

In terms of medical facilities, NEDA figures revealed an increase from 1,705 to 1,928 Rural Health Units (RHU) and a 100 percent increase in Barangay Health Units (BHU) from 1975 to 1980. There had been a steady decline, however, in the ratio of hospital beds to population, from 879 persons per hospital bed in 1974 to 1,573 by 1980. IBON noted that the proliferation of profit-oriented private hospitals and clinics made health services more inaccessible to the majority of the rural poor. Approximately 90 percent of the population do not have access to medical and health services and are disease-prone. The most common illnesses and causes of deaths are enumerated in Tables 16a and 16b.

Table 16a. Most Common Illnesses by Rank, Philippines, 1969-72 and 1982

TOP ILLNESSES	Rank in 1982	Rank in 1969-72
Influenza	1	1
Gastro-enteritis & other diarrheal diseases	2	2
Bronchitis	3	—
Accidents	4	—
Diseases of the heart	5	—
Tuberculosis, all forms	6	3
Pneumonia	7	4
Diseases of the vascular system	8	—
Mental disorders	9	—
Avitaminosis	10	—
Malignant neoplasms (cancers)	—	9
Malaria	—	5
Whooping cough	—	6
Measles	—	7
Dysentery, all forms	—	8
Infectious hepatitis	—	10

Sources. Bulletin Today, 10 January 1983, 1977 Philippine Statistical Yearbook, NEDA.

Table 16b. Top Causes of Death by Rank, Philippines, 1969-73 and 1982.

TOP CAUSES OF DEATH	Rank in 1982	Rank in 1969-73
Pneumonia	1	1
Diseases of the heart	2	3
Tuberculosis, all forms	3	2
Diseases of the vascular system	4	5
Malignant neoplasms (cancers)	5	7
Gastro-enteritis and colitis	6	4
Injuries	7	–
Accidents	8	6
Avitaminosis and nutritional deficiencies	9	9
Peptic ulcer	10	–
Bronchitis, emphysema and asthma	–	8
Congenital anomalies	–	10

Sources. Bulletin Today, 10 January 1983; 1977 Philippine Statistical Yearbook, NEDA.

Education

Educational level is an important factor in individual achievement as well as in national development. Income level determines education level and the latter determines the level of productivity and income. Two kinds of evidence show a close relationship between poverty and education. One is poverty incidence by the education levels of the household head and the other is the variation in regional poverty incidence and literacy ratio.

For 1982, poverty incidence fell almost continuously as the level of education rose for both urban and rural areas. The drop in poverty incidence was larger at each successive stages of education (i e. elementary school, high school, and college). Poverty incidence among those who did not complete any elementary education was lower than those who completed Grade V.

The adult literacy rate increased from 72% in 1960 to 88% in 1978. There was little difference between the literacy rates for women (86%) and men (87%) in 1975. However, the rural literacy rate of 79% was significantly lower than the urban rate of 93% in 1970.

Significant differences in literacy rates existed among various regions of the country in 1970. The literacy rate ranged from 65% in Western Mindanao to 90% in Central Luzon to 95% in Metro Manila. These differences may have narrowed subsequently since the overall literacy rate had increased from 84% in 1970 to 88% in 1978.

The high literacy rates are a function of the availability of schools and student participation rates. During schoolyear 1978-1979, there were 31,432 elementary schools accommodating 8.05 million students. The secondary schools numbered 4,617 and catered to 2.94 million students on a fee-paying basis.

Although enrollment rates were high at the elementary level, the dropout rates were likewise, high. Only 83% of the children entering school during schoolyear 1969-1970 reached Grade 2, 59% completed Grade 6, 46% proceeded to secondary school, and 34% completed secondary school.

A cause for some concern though is the quality of elementary education in the Philippines. A survey undertaken in 1974-75 found that the graduates of the elementary school had, on the average, absorbed only about 65% of the required materials, the major deficiencies being in reading, mathematics and language. They also suffered from a high level of 'functional illiteracy", i.e., an inability to read newspapers and comparable materials. The worst performance was in Mindanao, followed by Visayas while the best performance was in Central Luzon and Southern Tagalog.

NEDA statistics showed that total enrollment grew at an average annual growth rate of 3.3 percent from 12.6 million by SY 1980-81 to 13.4 million in SY 1983-84. Enrollment for 1984-85, however, registered a 1.1 percent-increase over the previous year.

Elementary enrollment did not increase substantially within the five-year (1980-81 to 1984-85) period with an average growth rate of only 1.08 percent. In contrast, secondary and tertiary enrollment grew at a faster rate of 2.64 percent and 5.3 percent, respectively, during the same period (Table 17).

Table 17. Enrollment by Levels, Philippines, 1980-1984.

SCHOOL YEAR	Elementary	Secondary	Tertiary	TOTAL
1980-81	8,290	3,013	1,276	12,579
1981-82	8,518	2,936	1,336	12,790
1982-83	8,591	2,957	1,412	12,960
1983-84	8,795	3,109	1,493	13,397
1984-85	8,960	3,230	1,540	13,730
Average Annual Growth Rate (In percent)				
1980-81	0.7	8.9	7.9	3.3
1981-82	0.7	2.5	4.7	1.7
1982-83	0.8	0.7	4.7	1.3
1983-84	2.4	5.2	5.7	3.4
1984-85	0.8	0.9	2.5	1.1
Average Growth Rate	1.08	2.64	5.3	2.16

Source of Basic Data: NEDA Statistical Coordination Office (SCO), *Economic and Social Indicators,* 1983. NEDA Philippine Developmental Report, 1984 (Draft)

Housing

It is difficult to estimate housing needs in the Philippines because of the rural concentration of the population and the questionable relevance of housing standards to the rural population.

The 1978-82 Philippine Development Plan stated that, in 1977, the national housing backlog reached 1,125,000 units. This means that in 1977, about 16% of the population was not adequately housed or not housed at all. The Plan projected a need for 2,261,400 new units by 1987.

While these figures included rural housing, the housing problem in the rural areas was considered to be less acute because of lower minimum standards and the ability of the rural population to construct its own housing. Urban areas, on the other hand, face the pressures of rapid urban population growth and the declining availability of service land for housing.

Thus in general, housing is more a problem of the poverty groups in the urban areas. While most rural households do not own their homelots, majority of them own their houses.

The urban poor, on the other hand, usually live in makeshift houses along esteros (estuaries) and riverbanks (8,250 families), along the Philippine National Railways tracks (6,000 families) and on government infrastructure sites (17,490 families). Metro Manila squatter families alone number 216,000.

A study conducted by the UP Institute of Social Work and Community Development (UP-ISWCD) reveals that squatter families cannot afford to pay for units provided by government housing program. A squatter family can only spend ₱7.50 to pay for housing rental. This is about three percent of the family's daily budget expenditures. *Business Day* observes that shelter has become a postponable need since the average Filipino household's disposable income allocated for shelter has now been rechanneled for food.

A related problem facing urban poor families is the constant threat and/or occurrence of demolition. A total of 11,312 families were evicted in Metro Manila from January 1982 to April 15, 1983. Less than half (5,000) of this number, however, have been accommodated in resettlement areas where facilities were inadequate and very little income-generating opportunities exist.

Water Supply and Sanitation

The World Health Organization (WHO) estimated that in 1975 about 43% of the Philippine population was served through the public water system, compared with 26% in 1970. Coverage from Metro Manila/Southern Tagalog was estimated at 81%, other urban areas 55% and rural areas 33% as compared to 77%, 70% and 27%, respectively in 1971.

Access of the population to safe water appeared to be relatively even for most regions, especially in rural areas. However, the urban populations of Cagayan Valley and Southern Mindanao, and the rural populations of Ilocos, Cagayan Valley, Central Luzon, and Central Mindanao had very low access to safe water. Most of the population not served by public water systems used unsafe sources of water such as shallow wells, springs and streams.

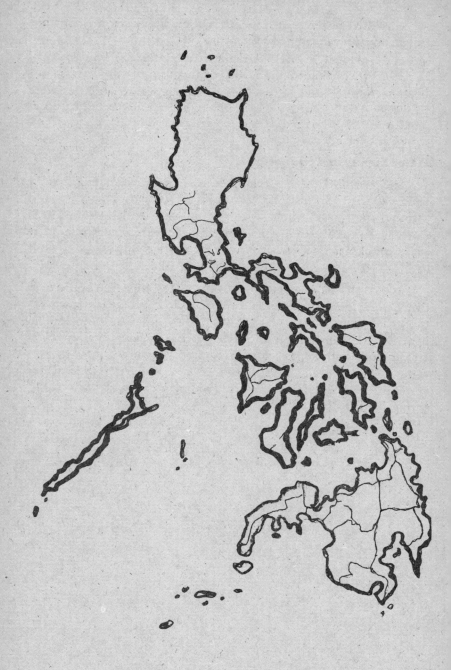

THE POVERTY GROUPS

While the use of a poverty threshold provides a gross index to gauge the magnitude of poverty, it does not advance one's understanding of what it means to be poor. For that, one has to look at who the poor are and the dynamics of their struggle for economic survival.

As mentioned earlier, the highest sectoral incidence of poverty is found in the agricultural labor force. The next highest incidence is among manual workers and the unemployed. Broken down into urban and rural, the highest incidence of poverty is found among manual workers in the urban areas. Of those considered poor in the agricultural sector, a large majority is engaged in farming and fishing. Among the urban poor, on the other hand, a large percentage falls in the category of craftsmen and production process workers. Unfortunately, there is no study on a national scale to segregate these categories further into distinct occupational groupings, thus, isolating poverty groups. This is partly due to a lack of a common definition of poverty and a common measurement standard for identifying poverty groups One has to rely on disparate data from micro studies undertaken in the search for identifying the poverty groups and for comparing their various levels of deprivation. This poses some problems as various researchers use different classification categories.

Aguilar used access to land and other productive assets as basis for classifying the rural poor, and the level of skills as the main criterion for the urban poor. He named the assetless poor as the most deprived of the poor groups in the rural area. This main group included the landless rice and corn farmers, the landless sugarcane workers (share tenancy and Hacienda workers), the landless coconut farm laborers, marginal fishermen, and the other assetless rural poor who work in other crops, i.e., tobacco, banana, and pineapple plantations. For the urban poor, Aguilar's classification included the stevedores, hawkers and vendors, and the scavengers.

33

The World Bank, on the other hand, based its classification on income derived from specific economic activities. Thus, their identified poor groups included the rice and corn growers, the sugarcane workers, and the marginal fishermen for the rural poor, and the laborers for the urban poor.

Meanwhile, the USAID simply "chose to distinguish the upland farmers, the paddy rice farmers, the landless agricultural workers, and the artisanal fishermen to portray the dynamics of rural poverty, and the informal sector workers for a glimpse at urban poverty.

Most researchers studied specific geographical areas in the country and tried to measure poverty incidence and levels of deprivation among identified sectoral groups (Kikuchi, Ledesma, Guerrero, etc.). The use of micro studies, therefore, as basis for identifying the poor groups is as subjective as the researcher's basic definition of poverty and his own value judgments as to what constitutes the poor. Furthermore, poverty trends are limited to the specific micro study and cannot be used for comparative purposes.

With these as limitations, the author has chosen the *resource base* from which families depend on as the main criterion for identifying poverty groups in the rural areas, and *income sources* for identifying the urban poor.

In the rural areas, farmers tend to have multiple sources of income and livelihood — both from farm and off-farm activities — thus, making it difficult to classify families according to distinct occupational groupings. The practice of intercropping, diversified farming, crop rotation, etc. makes it difficult to classify families according to subsectors or cropping patterns. The prevalence of small farm holdings which may or may not be viable depending on soil condition, use of appropriate technology, the size of the farm itself, tenancy conditions and crop mix are a poor determinant of poverty levels and incidence Classification of families and grouping them according to the resource base which the families manage and depend on for income cuts across occupational and sectoral groupings, multiplicity in the sources of income and livelihood, productivity and non-productivity of assets owned. Moreover, it facilitates the identification of opportunity areas for improving the socio-economic conditions of the poor.

Therefore, the poverty groups identified are the *landless rural workers* (dependence on the sale of their labor as their resource), the *upland farmers* (uplands as a resource base), the *lowland small owner-cultivators* (lowland farm) and the *artisanal fishermen* (sea).

For the urban poor, a different framework has to be used. Dependence on a resource base cannot be the key for the identification of the urban poor. For in the urban areas, the operative economic system is not agricultural but mainly industrial and tertiary sector-oriented. Thus, employable skills are the main assets required in an urban setting. Those with more technical and specialized skills have better job opportunities while those with minimal skills have limited employment potentials. Hence, the main criterion used for identifying the poor groups in the urban areas is the families' major source of income and livelihood. Using this as basis, it would appear that the *scavengers, hawkers/peddlers* and the *laborers* are the best representatives of the urban poor groups.

CONCLUSION AND RECOMMENDATIONS

Difficulties in defining poverty and in measuring its incidence stem from the varying definitions of poverty, the apparent arbitrariness of the measures used, and the inadequate data base from which an indepth analysis of poverty and its causes can be done. Using the three indices of income, food threshold and people's perception, poverty incidence in the Philippines was anywhere from 30 to 56 percent of the total population in 1971 (1.89 million to 3.53 million families); 64.3% (2.10 million to 4.51 million families) in 1975; and from 30 to 74 percent (2.72 million to 6.72 million families) in 1985. The trend seems to be that of increasing levels of poverty incidence and increasing inequality of income distribution among income classes and regions. Thus, it would appear that whatever economic growth the Philippines has experienced over the years has been of little benefit to the majority of the Filipino poor.

At least 78% of the poor families live in the rural areas. The regions with the highest incidence of poverty, both in the 1971 and 1975 FIES, are Northern Mindanao, Cagayan Valley, Bicol, Western Visayas and Eastern Visayas. Since the same regions have the highest poverty incidence in 1965, it would appear that there has been no improvement in the socio-economic conditions of these areas relative to the other regions in the country. In terms of percentage increase in poverty incidence, Metro Manila registered the highest increase between 1971 and 1975.

Cross-checking poverty incidence with the different regions' access to basic social services, it would appear that the poorer the regions (the higher the incidence of poverty), the less access to services they have. Causes for this imbalance have been cited as the unequal investment in public services among regions, concentration of development thrust and projects in the National Capital Region, and lack of government interventions in the provision of services. A cause for concern is the decreasing provision of adequate basic services to the regions.

The data also suggest a positive correlation between family size and poverty incidence; the bigger the family size, the

36

poorer the families tend to be. This is explained by high dependency ratios in poor families where one working member supports two or more dependents.

By occupation, the highest concentration of poor families were in the categories "farmers, fishermen, loggers and hunters" followed by "manual workers and laborers not elsewhere classified" in 1971. Unfortunately, there was no further breakdown of these occupational groupings to be able to compare the levels and incidence of poverty for each sub-group. The 1975 FIES had no breakdown of income distribution by occupational categories altogether. Thus, it is not possible to determine changes in poverty incidence by occupation over time.

Nevertheless, attempts at further segregating poverty data and isolating poverty groups have been made by various researchers. Micro studies have been undertaken specific to poverty groups in identified areas in the country. Using as basis the synthesis of micro studies and classifying the poor groups according to the resource base which they manage and depend on for income, the more disadvantaged groups in the rural areas are the landless rural workers, upland farmers, small owner-cultivators and the artisanal fishermen. For glimpses of urban poverty, micro studies suggest the scavengers, hawkers/peddlers and the laborers as representatives of the urban poor.

Both the rural and urban poor groupings tend to be modal types rather than discreet occupational groupings. Hence, they do not represent all the possible poor groups in the country today. Moreover, the studies tend to be more of a description of the various groups' characteristics, lifestyles, and survival strategies rather than attempts to measure their socio-economic well-being relative to other groups. Hence, there has been no study to compare changes in the economic and social well-being of the groups over time. These observations are partly due to the lack of common definition of poverty as well as uniform standard for measuring poverty incidence and levels. Thus, researchers tend to use their own definitions and construct their own measurement standards. Poverty trends and generalizations,

37

therefore, are limited to the specific micro study.

These findings highlight the following issues and concerns:

1. The need to adopt a common definition of, and a standard for measuring poverty incidence and in identifying poverty groups.

2. The need to monitor closely the changes in poverty incidence and levels using consistent and uniform measurement standards and research techniques/methodology. This means conducting time series studies on poverty and segregating data into specific categories consistently over time.

3. The need for the government to adopt *equity* as a development goal which is of equal importance as economic growth. This will mean implementation of programs and projects addressed towards minimizing inequality in the distribution of income, low productivity, imbalance among regions in the distribution of and access to services, facilities, and investments, unemployment, underemployment, and high population growth rates.

4. Among the sectors, the need to give priority to the primary health care system and rural water supply and sanitation facilities. The deficiencies are greatest in these areas and the per capita cost of improvement is rare. Although children and pregnant/nursing women emerge as the target groups which could benefit most from specific nutritional interventions, significant malnutrition appears to exist among the low-income groups. This can be most effectively addressed through increased incomes and a properly formulated food and nutrition program.

5. In education, the main priorities are reduction in the dropout rates at the elementary school level and improvement in the quality of elementary education.

Education can also play a significant role in supporting other basic services, such as health, nutrition, water supply and sanitation.

6. And lastly, the pervasiveness of poverty incidence in all regions of the country necessitates the need to harness the resources of both government and private agencies and individuals in addressing poverty issues and concerns. Special attention should be given to Northern Mindanao, Cagayan Valley, Bicol, Western Visayas and Eastern Visayas because of their high incidence of poverty and relatively less access to basic services, as well as Metro Manila because of the rapid increase in its poverty level over time.

CHAPTER 2
PHILIPPINE RURAL POVERTY

THE LANDLESS RURAL WORKERS

Who are the Landless Rural Workers?

In a 1978 workshop, the Philippine Council for Agriculture and Resources Research (PCARR) defined the landless rural worker as "one who works in agriculture but possesses neither ownership nor recognized rights to farm the land and who earns at least 50 percent of his income from the sale of his labor." The landless rural worker is inevitably subject to income shortfalls, mainly because of the "highly competitive and generally unremunerative setting" he works in (USAID 1980). Carner (1981) contends that the PCARR definition is not entirely adequate since it can include seasonal migrants who might have land elsewhere and are simply looking for work during the off-season.

In 1979, the Ministry of Labor and Employment conducted a study of landless rural workers in cooperation with the International Labor Organization. The study focused on four provinces, namely: Antique, Batangas, Negros Occidental and Iloilo. The study revealed that, on the average, landless agricultural workers are married, with a family size of 4-9 members. They have a mean age of 40-45 years and have reached some level of elementary schooling. Notably, most of the rural workers in Antique have worked as *sacadas* (migrant rural workers).

How Many Landless Rural Workers are There?

Aguilar (1981) noted that, in a span of a decade, the number of farm laborer families rose from 444,000 in 1961 to 703,000 in 1971. Their number grew by as much as 4.7 percent annually in contrast to the 0.96 percent annual growth of those classified as "self-employed" farming families.

Kikuchi (1983) posted a similar observation in his Laguna study where the number of landless households tripled from 23 percent of total village households in 1966 to 63 percent in 1980.

Based on census data, farm laborers in 1975 numbered 3.5 million representing about 47.5 percent of all agricultural workers in the country (Makil and Fermin 1978). The largest concentration of landless workers (or what Aguilar referred to as the assetless poor) was in the rice and corn subsectors (67 percent).

On the other hand, the Technical Board of Agricultural Credit (TBAC), in its preliminary report in 1978, gave a lower estimate of 1,150,000 landless rural workers. This was equivalent to 7.5 percent of the total labor force and 14.3 percent of the total number of persons employed in agriculture.

Carner (1981) tried to calculate the number of landless households based on the TBAC estimate. He came up with a "fair" estimate of 500,000 to 700,000 households considering that women workers constituted at most one-third of the agricultural worker population and that landless households have, at most, one child who was a laborer. In his study, Carner further distinguished the landless rural workers employed as farm laborers from those hired as plantation workers.

Both Aguilar and Carner agreed that farm workers in the rice-growing areas comprised the bulk of landless rural workers. Aguilar's study (1981) revealed further that the proportion of landless households at the village level could be anywhere between 20 to 50 percent. This holds true for 15 out of 21 study villages. It can be gleaned from these studies that landlessness is prevalent wherever rice is grown as a major crop.

Makil and Fermin (1978) reported that, in 1971, landless farm operators were predominantly found in Central Luzon, Southern Luzon, Western Visayas, Bicol and Southern Mindanao. Among the five provinces studied, Nueva Ecija had the biggest population of landless farm operators (70 percent) relative to the number of farm operators in the province. Laguna had a substantial 44 percent, Cebu, Negros Occidental and Quezon had about equal proportions (36, 37 and 37 percent, respectively).

LUSSA's (1982) study on peasants and fishermen in Bicol, Southern Tagalog and Ilocos sub-regions disclosed quite diverse

42

results in terms of concentration of landless workers by crops produced. Luzon Secretariat for South Action (LUSSA) found out that agricultural workers who neither own nor rent the land they farm constituted the bulk of sugar workers (59.49 percent). They were followed by tenants (35.69 percent) and small owner-cultivators (4.82 percent) (Table 18).

Table 18. Tenure Status of Sugar Workers, Philippines.

TENURE	Frequency	%
Tenants	111	35.69
Agricultural workers	185	59.49
Small Owner-Cultivators	15	4.82
Total	311	100.00

Source: LUSSA Research Staff (1982:212)

Table 19 shows that in the rice industry, share tenants (47.98 percent) comprised the majority in 1982[4]. Certificate of Land Title (CLT) holders constituted the least proportion (five percent).

Table 19. Tenure Status of Riceland Workers, Philippines.

TENURE STATUS	Frequency	%
Share Tenants	605	49.98
Leaseholders	215	17.05
Agricultural Workers	214	16.97
Small Owner-Cultivators	164	13.00
CLT Holders	63	5.00
TOTAL	1,261	100.00

Source: LUSSA Research Staff (1982:212)

---

[4]Kikuchi (1983) observed an annual rise of 14 percent in the value of tenancy titles in Laguna over a two-decade interval (1959-1980).

The disparity in proportion between agricultural workers in the rice industry and in the sugar industry (as shown in Tables 18 and 19) could be attributed to the fact that tenants and leaseholders in the rice industry have acquired rights to farm the land even if they are also landless.

How Poor are the Landless Rural Workers?

Ownership of Productive Assets

Studies conducted by the Philippine Peasant Institute (1985) in some selected Philippine regions disclosed that approximately 80 percent of the total 3,063,028 hectares of cropland in Mindanao were tilled by tenants, leaseholders, freeholding settlers or farmworkers. In the Visayas, about 70 percent of the estimated 2.5 million hectares were not owned by the actual producers. Similarly, in Central Luzon, 70 percent of rice farmers and 50 percent of sugar farmers remained landless.

In terms of ownership of productive assets other than land, Ledesma (1982) found out that landless workers consistently ranked last as compared to amortizing owners and permanent lessees. They generally did not own farm items except sickles, bolos and mats for grain drying.

Although bereft of productive assets, however, the landless farmer owns a temporary house usually constructed on a rent-free lot. In terms of housing facilities such as safe water sources and sanitary toilets, the landless are consistently inferior to farmers. Likewise, they are inferior with respect to ownership of consumer durables such as sewing machines. A relatively substantial number of landless households (49-63 percent), however, own transistor radio sets (Aguilar (1981).

Carner (1981) remarked that ownership of a carabao is an important asset as it significantly increases a laborer's wage rate or crop share. He also noted that since the landless rural workers have only their labor as their source of income, their health becomes a necessary asset given the highly competitive nature of their work environment.

Income

The landless rural workers are the most dependent on income derived from direct cultivation of the land. In the rice monoculture areas, landless workers are almost totally dependent on rice farmers for their employment and income. Based on Ledesma's study, the landless households derived 76 percent of their income as rice farm laborers. Officially legislated wage levels pegged the earnings of agricultural workers at a minimum of ₱39 in plantations and ₱30 outside plantations (IBON Facts and Figures as cited by PPI 1985). In practice, however, farm workers received only ₱10 to ₱15 average daily income.

Findings from one study revealed even lower wages for agricultural workers in the rice industry: 47.20 percent of agricultural workers earned ₱5 – ₱8 daily, while 19.16 percent of farm workers earned ₱9 – P12 daily. A small number (12.15 percent) earned a relatively higher ₱13 – ₱16 per day. In the sugar industry, majority (55.86 percent) earned an annual income of at least ₱3,000 or a minimum daily income of ₱8 (LUSSA 1982).

The LUSSA (1982) study also gave the proportion of production expenses devoted to wages of agricultural workers. In the rice industry, however, milling fees (54.86 percent) outnumbered both the wages of hired workers (17.07 percent) and the expense for agricultural inputs (15.33 percent). In the labor-intensive abaca and coconut industries, payment for agricultural workers constituted the bulk of production costs.

In 1980, the total household income of landless families was estimated at ₱2,000 to ₱3,000 per year (Carner 1981). Ledesma (1982) reported that in the 1977-78 dry season, the landless laborer in Iloilo earned ₱2,020 or 30 percent lower than rice farmers. Bautista and others (1983) found out that in Leyte, the Certificate of Land Title (CLT) holders had cash incomes twice as much as those of landless workers.

Generally, wages vary depending on the payment arrangement followed and the crops produced. Among farm laborers, share-croppers tend to earn more than wage earners. Among plantation workers, coconut laborers do better than sugarcane laborers, and permanent laborers receive more income than casual workers (Carner 1981).

In a study of sugar workers, for instance, the *dumaan* (resident workers) received the highest pay followed by the *pangayao* (transient workers) and the *sacada* (migrant workers) (Makil and Fermin 1978).

PPI (1985) also identified the prevailing "exploitative practices" such as the *sistemang prendes* and the *pakyawan.* Under prendes, the agricultural worker works in the planting or in the weeding process for free in order to be hired come harvest time. The sharing system usually used is the 7-6 system wherein the worker gets one sack of palay for every 7 sacks harvested. Prendes is also known as *gama* in Southern Luzon, *dumdum* or *sundonan* in Mindanao and *atorga* in Northern Luzon.

Under the pakyawan system, like in the Visayas, the agricultural worker is paid a fixed wage (usually ₱500 per hectare) for the whole process of replanting, pulling of weeds and harvesting. Pakyawan is also called *patasan* or *pakyaw-tanum.*

According to Aguilar, landless workers in rice farms appear to earn considerably less than their counterparts in other crop areas. As a case in point, rice farm workers in Laguna (of whom 78 percent are landless) earn ₱785 annually at 1972 prices. This is 17 percent less than those earned by workers in rice-coconut or rice-sugarcane fields (79 percent landless) and 43 percent lower than the earnings of coconut farm laborers (93 percent landless) (Table 20).

Table 20. Mean Annual Income of Farm Workers in Selected Provinces and Crop Areas, at Current and Constant 1972 Price.

PROVINCE/CROP/YEAR	Worker's Annual Income		Investi-gator
	Current Prices	Constant 1972 Prices*	
Negros Occidental (1982)			Gonzaga (1983)
Sugar cane			
Skilled Workers (N=49)	₱6,361	₱1,708	
Unskilled Workers (N=104)	₱3,750	₱1,077	
Laguna (1973)			Wickhan, Torres, Castillo (1974)
Rice (N=69)	915	785	
Rice-coconut/Rice-sugar (N=33)	1,106	949	
Coconut (N = 28)	1,604	1,377	

*Current prices deflated by the national CPI with 1972 as base year.

Source: Aguilar (1983:14).

In a more recent study conducted by Gonzaga (1983) in Negros Occidental, the individual income of rice farm laborers is lower by 22 percent than that of the unskilled laborers, and 54 percent less than that of the skilled sugarcane farm workers.

Notably, differences within rice-growing areas also existed. Landless laborers who depended purely on wages earned in non-farm activities were significantly better-off than those who depended wholly or in part on wages earned in the agricultural sector (Bautista 1977). As Table 21 shows, a worker engaged in purely agricultural work earned 61 percent less than one engaged in purely non-agricultural work and 37 percent less than one with mixed jobs.

Table 21. Comparative Socio-Economic Indicators for Different Types of Landless Workers, Barangay Sta. Lucia, Sta. Ana, Pampanga, Philippines, 1977.

TYPE OF LANDLESS WORKER	Mean Annual Income (₱)	Mean Debt (₱)	Mean No. of Days Worked	% of Year Worked (Base = 240)
Worker engaged in purely agricultural work	1,042	507.50	105	44
Worker engaged in mixed jobs	1,651	572.73	138.5	58
Worker engaged in purely non-agricultural work	2,660	400.00	167	69

Source: Bautista (1977).

Most agricultural workers are employed only during planting and harvesting seasons. In between peak seasons, they engage in duck raising and piggery, handicraft making, vending, fishing, and carpentry. Opportunities for supplementary income appear greatest for farm laborers, secondly for coconut workers, and lastly, for sugar plantation laborers (Carner 1981). Income from these sources make up one-fourth of the landless households' total income or roughly ₱500 per year (TBAC 1978).

On expenditure patterns, Ledesma (1982) and Makil and Fermin (1978) observed that landless households spent a greater proportion of their income on food. Ledesma found out that the landless workers of Iloilo and Nueva Ecija spent 66 percent of their income on food while rice farmers spent only 55 percent.

Access to Services

As Ledesma's study in Iloilo and Nueva Ecija showed, landless workers had less access to social services such as education. Enrollment patterns revealed that the school enrollment ratios for children of farmer and landless households in the 7-12 age group were both high, but the gap widened for the higher age groups.

Unlike their farmer counterparts, the landless workers have no access to commercial credit sources due to lack of collateral. They cannot even qualify for membership in the Samahang Nayon because they cannot meet the organization's requirements. Even the Land Reform Program did not include the landless laborers (Ledesma 1982). Hence, the landless have no other alternative but to rely on relatives, neighbors and friends or even money lenders for their credit needs which, for the most part, are allocated for consumption rather than for production.

Organizational Membership

Practically all of the landless respondents in Ledesma's study were not members of either the Samahang Nayon or Compact Farmers since they did not own lands.

Kerkvilet (1983) enumerated three factors which hinder landless laborers from organizing themselves, namely:

1. Direct and/or indirect repression;
2. The division among workers arising from stiff competition and unwillingness to severities with landlord-patrons by overtly aligning with others; and
3. The view held by the landless that they are solely responsible for their own predicament.

Despite these hindrances, 33 provincial peasant organizations exist in the country (Philippine Peasant Institute 1985). PPI also observed a remarkable growth in the number of peasant groups and intensity of the open mass movement. It projected that the thrust of the peasant movement for the next three years would revolve around two major factors: (1) organizing and consolidating a national peasant coalition; and (2) initiating sustained, nationally coordinated peasant campaigns.

Why are They Landless?

At the macro-level, Aguilar (1981) identified three factors which have precipitated landlessness: (1) the slow growth and capital-intensive nature of industrial development failed to create new jobs for an annual increment of 500,000 persons; (2) population growth remained high despite a slight annual decline of about three percent; and (3) the highly unequal structure in the ownership and distribution of land.

At the micro level, two factors cause landlessness: (a) displacement from the land; and (2) impoverishment of farming households. Aguilar attributed both factors to the Green Revolution Program which favored the capital-intensive over the labor-intensive production system. The shift to mechanized farming also ejected most farmers from the lands they till except for a few who have the skills in operating these machines. Thus, Aguilar concluded that while the Green Revolution increased farm yields and total output, it "has, in fact, favored the already relatively well-off."

Moreover, the Land Reform Program failed to rectify land distribution not only because many landowners have been able to circumvent the law but basically because it has a very limited coverage. For one, as Ledesma (1982) observed, landless rural workers who could have been one of the primary targets of the program were excluded in its scope. Moreover, the program exempted farms devoted to export crops such as coconut, sugar, abaca, and fruit trees, thus, favoring not only the local big landowners but also their foreign counterparts.

PPI (1985) also identified "land monopoly" as the principal cause of landless. This is perpetuated by outright landgrabbing using the twin tactics of deception and coercion. Even more disturbing is the perpetuation of land monopoly through

50

certain government policies and programs which tend to favor the interests of the big landlords and foreign capitalists at the expense of the landless peasant households.

PPI asserts that land grabbing is an "effective means of seizing control over already occupied lands." It intensified rapidly under the Export-Oriented Industrialization (EOI) strategy as a result of the agricultural incentives offered to both foreign and local agribusiness corporations. The Corporate Farming Program implemented in 1975 likewise provided favorable conditions for corporate access to peasant lands. As of 1981, 1,267 corporations and 95 corporate farms were able to acquire a total of 86,017 hectares (Sison as cited by PPI 1985).

Citing statistics from the Ministry of Agrarian Reform (Table 22) and *Bulletin Today* (Table 23), PPI deduced that the Land Reform Program had failed and had only resulted in the expropriation of small holdings by big landlords, bureaucrats, and transnational corporations (TNCs).

Table 22. Emancipation Patents* Summary: Operation Land Transfer, Program Accomplishment as of June 30, 1972.

CERTIFICATE OF LAND TRANSFER	SCOPE	ACCOM-PLISHMENT	%
No. of tenants involved	396,082	438,670	110.75
No. of certificates	556,114	582,441	104.73
Hectarage involved	730,734	678,973	92.92
EMANCIPATION			
No. of tenants		2,352	0.59
No. of patents		3,221	0.58
Area involved		1,923	0.26

Source: Ministry of Agrarian Reform Accomplishment Report, June 1982.

*MAR grants emancipation patents only after two consecutive amortizations.

Table 23. Emancipation Patents as of June 1984

EMANCIPATION PATENTS	ACCOM-PLISHMENT	%
No. of tenants	103,155	26.04
No. of patents	116,979	21.03
Area involved	112,445	1.76

Source: Bulletin Today (July 22, 1984).

In the same view, the Integrated Area Development (AID) Strategy resulted in the massive dislocation of peasant communities from their farm lands in exchange for infrastructure components such as dams, ports, roads, and bridges (PPI 1985). The eviction of peasants in Cagayan, Samar and Zamboanga, among others, to give way for the Cagayan IADP, the Samar Integrated Rural Development Project and the Zamboanga del Sur Integrated Development Project illustrate the "land grabbing" nature of these programs (PPI 1985).

PPI also noted the reformation projects which systematically uprooted upland farmers and settler families. The PPI report cited PD 1705 and PD 1559 as the legal basis of these reforestation schemes. In Central Visayas alone, reforestation covers 81,141 hectares.

PPI also cited the recently-launched Balanced Agro-Industrial Development (BAID) Strategy as being extremely prejudicial to land ownership by the small farmers. In analyzing BAID, PPI asserts that "virtually circumvents" the Land Reform Program since it exempts lands planted to other crops from being converted to rice and corn lands and, thus, from being subjected to land reform. This encourages local and foreign corporations to enter into the production of non-traditional crops, particularly yellow corn.

Conclusion and Recommendations

Having limited access to land and other productive assets, the landless rural worker is one of the poorest of the poor groups in the rural areas. With only two to three years of education and with no employable skills, they depend on the sale of their labor for their subsistence. Family, community and plantation ties provide them with sources of employment which are often seasonal. Thus, they receive wages which can buy only one-half of the minimum food requirements for himself and his family. With no cash surplus, they do not own assets which can be used as collaterals for credit purposes. Having to constantly look for means to subsist, they are unorganized and unpoliticized; thus, they become victims of exploitative and unfair labor and marketing practices.

The above conditions of the landless rural workers is aggravated at the macro level by the following conditions which further preclude them from acquiring a piece of land: growing population, increasing fragmentation of land, spread of large commercial plantation, and eviction of tenants by landowners opposed to land tenure in rice and corn areas. Consequently, the option of the landless seem to be limited to the following:

1) Searching for unclaimed land;
2) Paying a premium for tenancy rights;
3) Subsisting on tiny fragments of land;
4) Migrating to growth areas; and
5) Remaining as farm hands in **small-farm** holdings, plantation agriculture, or as domestic helpers for relatively well-off families

The first option has resulted to the current trend of migration to the uplands but even there, land security has become a problem. The second option is reflected in the use of the *puesto*, a premium for farming rights paid by an outgoing tenant. Takahashi reports that, in 1972, the *puesto* for a one-hectare field suitable for double cropping was around ₱2,500 to ₱3,000. In 1980, it was reported that the price of tenancy title amounted to ₱14,250 per hectare in the Laguna area (Kikuchi 1983).

Considering the income level of the landless and the unavailability/scarcity of credit sources, the landless rural worker's family cannot afford to pay the price.

Land fragmentation, as the third option, is seen in the proliferation of small farms. Farms of less than two hectares in size constituted 41% of all rice farms in 1960. But by 1972, these farms constituted 69% of the total area planted to rice. At the same time, the corresponding average area for these farms declined from 0.93 to 88.0 hectare (IBRD 1976). However, a piece of farm land has to be at least three hectares to be economically viable (WB 1980). Therefore, further land fragmentation is not a feasible option to improve the lot of the landless. On the other hand, the outright purchase of farm holdings does not pose as an alternative because if tenancy rights cannot be paid off, the landless rural worker cannot afford to purchase and own a piece of land.

Without ownership nor tenancy rights to the land, the landless rural workers migrate to cities and other growth areas in search for better employment opportunities. But with the very low absorptive capacity of the industrial sector, the landless rural workers end up doing menial jobs as stevedores and laborers, or they engage in scavenging, and peddling or join the ranks of the urban unemployed. With no regular and adequate income, they live in makeshift houses and stay in rent-free lands, thus, further exacerbating the highly congested and blighted conditions in the slum areas. To ignore the plight of the landess would mean some 700,000 households living in absolute poverty. With a growth rate of four percent per annum, this number would simply be too large to ignore.

Given the above scenario, the following interventions seem to be warranted to improve the conditions of the landless rural workers:

1. Enabling the landless rural workers to gain access to, or own, a piece of arable land. Several schemes are possible:
   - Land Transfer
   - Land Distribution
   - Land Use/Leasehold Arrangements

Concomitant with these schemes are the simultaneous provision of financial assistance to enable the family to start farm operations and market their produce, as well as training and technical assistance in the use of appropriate farm technologies. Thus, the schemes call for the transformation of the landless from just being laborers or farm hands to producers of their own crops. In addition to the implementation of the above schemes is the re-examination of the existing policies and programs which tend to favor monopolies and the interests of big landlords at the expense of the landless peasant households (e.g., corporate farming, integrated area development, agro-forestry and land reform).

2. Finding alternative employment for the landless rural worker and his family. Rural industries can be established and skills training activities geared towards industry needs can be undertaken. Rural industries will provide the landless rural workers with regular sources of income, thus, preventing their migration to urban cities and other growth areas. Furthermore, it will save the LRW from a life of marginal subsistence to a level where he can send his children to school, purchase minimum food requirements for himself and his family, and have enough savings for the future.

3. Providing the landless rural workers and his family with secondary sources of income. Possible income-generating activities include swine and poultry raising, vegetable gardening, carabao raising, trading, etc. These activities will entail the provision of seed capital, training, and technical assistance in the production, marketing and financial management of these activities. Provision of capital to the landless assumes outright grant or loans through social credit schemes.

4. Providing the landless rural workers with "integrated basic social services," i.e., education, health, water and sanitation. This implies the allocation and re-channeling of resources to the regions of the country where there is a bigger concentration of the poor. Furthermore, it assumes an effective and efficient mechanism for the delivery of services.

5. Organizing the landless rural workers into a cohesive economic and political unit able to articulate their needs and work for the improvement of their socio-economic well-being.

THE UPLAND FARMERS

Who are the Upland Farmers?

Upland farmers are mostly subsistence farmers of marginal land on rolling hills and steep mountain slopes (USAID 1980). They usually grow rice, corn and other rootcrops in very marginal farms which often have eroded and depleted soils. Their farms are generally located in areas with some degree of slope (i.e., at lands which are capable of holding less rain water) (Jimenez and Francisco 1984, Aguilar 1982).

Various researchers have classified the upland farmers in different ways. Sevilla classified uplanders into tribal or ethnic communities and migrant settlers from the lowlands. Duldulao (1978) categorized ·kaingeros (slash-and-burn cultivators) into three types: (1) born kaingero; (2) forced kaingero; and (3) speculator kaingero. Dozina and Herdt (1973 as cited in Carner 1981) categorized upland farmers into: (1) indigenous kaingero; (2) marginal kaingero; and (3) upland rice and corn farmers.

In his review of available data, Sevilla found out that upland ethnic communities practice kaingin as a necessary adaptive cultural practice. Inasmuch as kaingin-making fosters a shifting or semi-sedentary way of life, tribal communities tend to maintain their small size and predominantly kinship-based structure (Sajise 1981).

Basically, the marginal kaingeros treat their kaingin farms as "a production technology to derive economic benefits" (Ganapin 1979). They usually raise cash crops consciously, avoiding perennial crops due to insecurity of land tenure. Ignorant, if not unmindful, of the ecological effects of their farming practices, the migrant settlers have converted their area into cogon land within a span of three years (Olofson 1981, Sajise 1981).

Profile of Upland Farmers

Sajise (1981) argued that upland communities are generally small in size because their subsistence economy and relative physical mobility cannot support larger population.

Duldulao (1981) suggested that kaingeros born of kaingero parents, whether tribal or migrant, rely solely on kainginmaking for their survival. Hence, they exercise more restraint in their utilization of upland resources. Forced kaingeros, on the other hand, resort to kaingin-making due to poverty. Speculator kaingeros are wealthy families who are motivated by the desire to accumulate more wealth out of the forest resources. The last two groups practice what Olofson calls "disharmonic swidden practices" which are beyond the control of a traditional technological and religious system.

Dozina and Herdt's (ca. 1973) classification described the indigenous kaingero as an illiterate, non-Christian farmer who subsists on various crops suitable for annually shifting cultivation, produced on remote, "illegally-occupied", tropical rain forest (Ganapin 1979). Marginal kaingeros are mostly literate, Christian farmers who have migrated from the lowlands. Seventy percent of their income is derived from annual and perennial crops produced by slash-and-burn/weed-and-burn operations on marginal accessible forest, bush and grasslands, generally recognized as agricultural rather than forest reserves. Upland rice and corn farmers rely on plowed, rolling-slope land to usually produce corn in the dry season and rice in the wet season (Carner 1981).

Data from the CDSS FY 1982 indicated that indigenous kaingeros have the least formal education, followed by marginal kaingeros with at most three years of education. Upland rice and corn farmers registered the higher educational attainment of four years on the average. Educational opportunities for children and their concomitant upward social mobility continued to be limited because of the irregular demands of kainginmaking and the off-farm employment of upland rice and corn households.

Meanwhile, the study of Samonte and others on the Pantabangan upland community in 1980 revealed that 84.75 percent were married. Ganapin's (1979) data from five non-ethnic kaingin settlements showed that 64.97 percent of kaingeros have dependents. These two studies reflected Duldulao's (1977) findings that since the majority of upland males are family men, they place the family's welfare over and above communal interests.

Where are the Upland Farmers?

Geographically, the Philippines is 60 percent upland (Aguilar 1982). Lamberte identified 20 upland provinces in the Philippines. These include: Benguet, Mountain Province, Ifugao, Kalinga-Apayao, Antique, Eastern Samar, Northern Samar, Southern Leyte, Basilan, Agusan del Norte, Agusan del Sur, Bukidnon, Surigao del Sur, Davao Oriental, and Zamboanga del Sur.

Lamberte recorded that the biggest concentration of kaingin households is in Bukidnon (12,550), followed by Benguet (8,743), Agusan del Sur (5,271) and Surigao del Sur (5,184). The least number is in Basilan (124), Zambales (358) and Aklan (630).

How Many are They?

Alvarez (1981) estimated the upland population at between 4-6 million. The Bureau of Forest Development (BFD) — Upland Development Working Group gave a higher figure of 7.5 million, of which 4.5 million are national cultural communities.

Based on the BFD Census of Forest occupants, about 173,622 marginal kaingero families occupied the uplands as of 1982. Assuming an average family size of five to six members, Lamberte (1983) calculated that upland population was approximately 834,225 to 1,001,190. Carner (1981), on the other hand, estimated that there were 500,000 kaingero families as reflected in the BFD census in 1972. These varying estimates tend to confirm the nomadic nature of upland households.

How Poor are the Upland Farmers?

Ownership of Productive Assets

For tribal uplanders, land ownership is theoretically assured by law and is typically inherited from parents or relatives who have previously claimed the land by right of usage. The work performed in clearing the forest and in cultivating the land is perceived as sufficient proof of ownership (Olofson 1981, Bernales and de la Vega 1982).

Upland migrants, on the other hand, exercise various types of land ownership. Lowlanders resettled to the mountains by the government because of development projects (e.g., Panta-bangan Dam in Nueva Ecija) may be owner-tillers, share tenants, or lessees (Sevilla). Like the tribal minorities, some kaingeros also practice right of usage, while others purchase the farm from other kaingeros (Ganapin 1979). Lands may also be acquired through title purchase, homesteading through temporary per-mits from the BFD or verbal agreements with the landowner.

The size of upland farms ranges from 0.5 to 25 hectares with an average size of three hectares. The actual cultivated land, however, averages only one hectare (Olofson 1981, Tapawan 1981, Aguilar 1982, Bernales and de la Vega 1982).

Most kaingeros own some farm implements and livestock. Majority of upland rice and corn farmers possess more non-land assets than kaingeros. These assets include small-scale capital goods such as hand tractors and hand threshers.

Sevilla noted that upland farmers generally still use tradi-tional agricultural implements mainly because of the prohibitive cost of modern tools and inputs. Uplanders perceive that tradi-tional methods are more suitable to the upland soil and ter-rain. In addition, they lack technical information and access to market places. Farm tools and implements used include the bolo, dibble stick, hoe, hatchet, axe, sickle, trowel and spade. Sevilla cited Aguilar (1982) and Bernales and de la Vega (1982) when she mentioned that the majority of upland farmers use carabaos.

Income

Lamberte (1983) observed that 17 out of the 20 identified up-land areas belonged to the NEDA roster of distressed or less de-veloped areas within the country. His computations revealed that upland provinces have relatively low income, whether in terms of total household income, average household income or average per capita income.

Abrera (1976), as cited by Sevilla, concluded that based on economic indicators, the great majority of upland families fell below the poverty threshold as well as the 1974 food threshold for absolute poverty of ₱4,643 for rural households. Based on several studies cited by Sevilla, some upland areas especially project or resettlement sites — tend to record an annual average income of above ₱3,000.

Comparing upland farm incomes with expenditures tends to result in deficits. Floro's study on Pantabangan resettled households in 1981 showed that household needs exceeded gross income by about ₱1,000. Together with Tapawan (1981) and de Raedt (1982), Floro also found out that much of the household expenses were channeled to food purchased at the market place, crop inputs, household needs and education. Savings, if any, are very minimal.

Most of the upland farmers' income were in the form of root-crops and some upland rice which was largely consumed by the household. UNDP/FAO data showed that on the average, five tons per hectare of poor crops and 0.4 m.t. per hectare of upland rice were produced (UNDP/FAO n.d.)

Marginal kaingeros, in general had higher incomes because they had greater access to markets for cash crops. Income estimates for upland rice and corn farmers was ₱3,500 in 1974. Notably, tenants and subsistence white corn farmers earned lower than mixed rice and cash corn farmers.

Nutritional Status

Findings showed that upland farmers suffer from nutritional deficiencies owing to the low nutritional content of upland subsistence crops and limited cash to buy food. Differentials in nutritional status between kaingeros and migrant uplanders also exist. Because of their greater access to lowland services and relatively greater opportunities for cash earnings, it can be deduced that lowland migrants are assured of a greater quantity of food.

61

Coping Mechanisms

Owing to the inadequacy of marginal lands to provide enough production for subsistence needs, uplanders usually seek secondary sources of income, such as rattan-gathering, firewood and handsown timber, gum, coal, abaca (hemp) stripping, piecework on lowland farms and copra-making (UNDP/FAO n.d.). Housewives and other household members contribute about 25 percent of the total household income from off-farm sources.

Sevilla (ca. 1983) noted that a few households engaged in livestock and poultry-raising, reserving some of their animals for home consumption during rituals, feasts and other special occasions. The rest of the livestock were traded or sold for cash. Handicrafts formerly used exclusively for household consumption were also transformed into secondary sources of income. Products included blankets, pottery, brooms, bead work, carvings, baskets and mats. Also sold were such forest products as fuelwood, ferns, orchids, mushrooms and honey (e.g. Kikuchi 1971, Noval-Morales and Moran 1979).

Jimenez and Francisco (1984), in their study of the rural poor in Leyte, identified the upland farmers' major survival strategies as follows: raising other crops and livestock: working as hired hands for other farmers; carpentry and other related work; tricycle, jeepney and tractor driving in the lowlands; and tuba and bamboo gathering.

Aside from providing additional manpower in farmwork, women also engage in handicraft making such as hat and mat weaving and abaca rope making. A proportion of the younger population helps augment the household income by migrating to other villages or in urban centers to work in service-related jobs, usually as household help.

Why are they Poor?

The major constraints affecting kaingeros and upland farmers, as identified by the CDSS FY 1982, include the following: (1) increasing population pressures on the resource base caused by high fertility and in-migration; (2) declining productivity as a result of over-planting, inappropriate methods of farming and the absence of irrigation, terracing and other land improvements; (3) low level of education and skills; (4) lack of effective organization; (5) inaccessibility to markets; and (6) seasonal agricultural employment and limited alternative employment opportunities.

Conclusion and Recommendations

Upland farmers are mostly subsistence farmers of marginal lands on rolling hills and steep mountain slopes. Their access to land provides them with a source for their daily subsistence and some marketable surplus to generate cash for other household needs. In addition, they raise some livestock and engage in wage labor to further augment their cash earnings. Despite these resources, the estimated household income for all upland farmers fall below the poverty threshold of ₱5,201 in 1975, the estimated average household income being ₱3,500. This is slightly higher than the estimated income range for the landless rural workers (₱2,000-₱3,000). Various studies cited the following reasons: the physical inaccessibility of the uplands, the control of market mechanisms by lowland merchants, and the non-existence of markets that would absorb the upland farmers' household surplus. More basic problems confronting the upland farmers are the insecurity of land tenure, declining productivity as a result of over-exploitation, inappropriate methods of farming, absence of irrigation, terracing, and other land improvements, and the increasing population pressures on the resource base caused by high fertility and in-migration. Faced with these problems, the upland farmers tend to look for alternative sources of income from the lowlands as agricultural laborers, hired hands in fishing vessels, or as participants in informal trading activities. With their low level of skills and low educational attainment, their productive activities are seasonal in nature, and more often they become victims of unfair labor and marketing practices.

In addition to the concerns for upgrading the socio-economic conditions of the upland farmers is the consequent protection and conservation of the upland resource base.[5] Land uses that result in soil erosion and forest destruction are the major threats to water supply and quality, coastal eco-system, wildlife populations, and other environmental quality indicators. These resources are the basic source of livelihood of the poor groups and once the point of irreversible environmental decline is reached, any progress in development attained in the interim will be gradually, but inexorably, lost.

The intervention opportunities, therefore, are as follows:

1. Granting of security of land tenure for upland farmers. This includes land registration and legitimization of unofficially cultivated lands. This measure will greatly help stabilize population and increase investments in the uplands.

The Government's Social Forestry Program is a measure towards this end. Stewardship contracts are drawn up with individual upland farmers who then can avail of a twenty-five year-lease of the land renewable for another twenty-five years. The provision states that the upland farmers would only undertake activities that would lead to conservation of upland resources and would enhance the environmental stability of the area. The major drawback, however, is that farmers want titles to their land so that they can assure their children of an inheritance. The coverages of the Social Forestry Program is also limited by the fact that areas to timber, pulpwood, pasture, and other concessionaires are excluded. It is precisely in these areas however, where concessionaires and large-scale government projects have entered, where land security is most intense. Thus, a re-examination of the program is warranted.

Another area which should be looked into is the pattern of ownership among cultural communities. A system whereby traditional concepts of ownership and the formal registration and issuance of titles to land can be integrated should be looked into.

---

[5]See Appendix B (Philippine Environmental Profile).

2. Increasing upland productivity and income through:

   a. The introduction and use of appropriate agriculture and forestry production technologies, e.g., soil and nutrient conservation, tools and farm equipment, proper crop-mix, etc.

   b. Physical infrastructure development, e.g., roads, drainage, water impounding facilities, etc.

   c. Access to markets to facilitate marketing of produce, thus, generating additional cash income for the household.

   d. Training of farmers in the use and application of appropriate agriculture and forestry production technologies.

   e. Credit assistance to start farm operations, purchase farm inputs and implements.

3. Provision of secondary sources of income for the upland farmer and his family. Examples of these are livestock raising, vegetable gardening, handicraft-making, etc. Corollary to this is the provision of training, technical and financial assistance to the upland farmer and his household.

4. Organization of upland farmers into an effective economic and political unit able to identify, prioritize, and work for the solution and satisfaction of their problems and needs. This subsumes value orientation, the development of an appreciation and concern for the uplands and the country as a whole. In addition, a commitment to participate in community/group activities.

5. Provision of integrated basic social services in upland communities, e.g., health units, schools, water and sanitation facilities, extension programs and other community services. This implies not only re-channeling and allocation of resources towards the uplands but likewise the development of an appropriate and inter-agency machinery that would make the efficient delivery of services possible.

6. Implementation of strong measures to stop destructive logging, promote replanting and protect open upland areas.

THE ARTISANAL FISHERMEN

Who are the Artisanal Fishermen?

Artisanal fishermen are variably referred to as municipal, small-scale, subsistence, or sustenance fishermen. They use gears which either do not require boats or which require boats of not more than three tons. Their boats are the traditional outrigger type known as *bancas*. They operate in inland and marine waters within three nautical miles from the municipal coastline, although they can actually operate farther than three miles from shore if they used motorized bancas (Jimenez and Francisco 1984, Ardales and David 1984, USAID 1980).

The fishing industry employs about five percent of the country's total labor force. Of the total population of 47 million, 2.2 million depend on fish for their livelihood. About 795,000 people depend directly on fish production: 45,000 on commercial fishing, 574,000 on municipal fishing, and 176,000 on inland fishing (i.e., handling shore facilities, working in fishponds and engaging in oyster farming) (LUSSA Research Staff 1982).

Holazo (1979) recorded that the nearly 600,000 municipal fishermen in the country are located in 10,000 coastal fishing villages nationwide. Almost half of these fishermen are found in Southern Tagalog, Bicol, Eastern and Central Visayas, and Western Mindanao (Smith and others n.d.).

While municipal fishermen comprise 72.2 percent (574,000) of the total fishing industry (based on LUSSA's estimate), they only produce less than one million metric tons (1.67 metric tons per municipal fisherman). In contrast, commercial fishermen who comprise a lower 5.66 percent recorded an output of 11.2 metric tons per person , six times greater than that of the municipal fisherman (LUSSA 1982).

In 1979, municipal fishing comprised the major bulk of total fish production (59.83 percent of the national output). Notwithstanding its major contribution to the national output, municipal fishing's productivity remains very low. The Food and Agriculture Organization (FAO) estimates that only 80 percent of coastal fish and marine resources had been exploited by municipal fishing (Ibid).

Carner (1981) included the sustenance fishermen in his classification of the poorest occupational groups in Philippine society. Their low productivity is partly due to their use of traditional fishing technology. While they do not show the use of modern fishing technology and equipment, they simply do not have the means to acquire and, thereafter, maintain modern fishing paraphernalia (Jimenez and Francisco 1984).

How Poor are the Artisanal Fishermen?

Ownership of Productive Assets

A fishing unit consists of a fishing craft, usually the banca and gear. The banca is equipped with an outrigger for stabilization and measures between three to seven meters long (LUSSA 1982). The volume of the catch, the number of fishermen needed in a fishing boat and other factors depend upon the kind of fishing gear available for use.

Ownership of particular types of fishing equipment largely determines the income within a fishing community. There is a positive correlation between income and ownership of these productive assets, especially the vessel.

According to Carner (1981), 74 percent of the municipal fishermen own fishing gear. These include hand-held instruments, barriers and traps, set lines and nets. Sixty percent of the fishermen do not own bancas. They, therefore, rent bancas, act as crew for banca owners, are hired as laborers on larger crafts, rafts fish with hooks and lines, or net fish on shorelines.

Income

Carner also reports that distribution of the catch generally, and has traditionally, revolved around families and interpersonal ties. The net income is divided between the banca owner and the rest of the crew, with the former usually getting at least half of the share. Although the sharing system generally revolves around a mutual concern for everybody's welfare, the fishing laborer who owns neither vessel nor gear tends to receive the lowest share.

Carner foresees that as resources dwindle and capital costs increase, the nature of social relationships between the banca owner and the fishermen will shift from obligatory to contractual arrangement, thus, forcing the poorest fishermen with the least resources to find alternative income sources. This eventually poses another difficulty since the fishermen possess very limited productive assets. Less than 20 percent own lands of less than two hectares. Likewise, very few own any household asset, although 90-95 percent own their houses.

Dependency on the middlemen in marketing their produce further aggravates the plight of the fishermen. Although the catch can be sold directly to consumers, the fishermen tend to reserve the better grades of fish for the wholesalers. This buyer-seller relationship is popularly known as *suki*. The wholesaler acts as guarantor of purchase and also as source of credit. While *suki* has mutually beneficial aspects, fishermen often end up indebted to middlemen and banca owners and have expressed an interest in alternative marketing arrangements (Smith and others n.d.).

Another factor which limits the income of sustenance fishermen is the seasonality of fishing. In Southern Leyte, for example, fishermen consider it very risky to fish from June to August when waves are usually large. Moreover, the fishermen have to contend with natural calamities which not only results in lack of catch but also in damages to property (PBSP n.d.).

LUSSA (1982) pegged the fishermen's daily income from ₱5 to ₱15 on an irregular basis. In one month, for instance, the vessel fishes for only 12-15 days with one fishing trip lasting from one night to two and a half days. The number of fishing days do not guarantee a sizeable fish catch. During bad weather or after a trawler has swept the fishbed, the fishermen usually return with little or no catch at all. The peak months are December to May while the lean months are June to November.

Coping Mechanisms

Similar to the other poverty groups, artisanal fishermen are compelled to find other sources of income in order to survive. Southern Leyte fishermen, for instance, derive part of their income from coconut and other farm crops (PBSP n.d.). Seventy percent of the respondents in the LUSSA study (1982) from Bicol, Southern Tagalog and Ilocos sub-regions had other sources of income. These include domestication of animals, vegetable planting and small-scale business, i.e., *sari-sari* store.

Fishermen also resort to borrowing in order to provide for their household and production needs. In the same study undertaken by LUSSA, 80.06 percent of the respondents admitted that they had outstanding debts. More than half of the sustenance fishermen's loans (60.1 percent) were reportedly used for their basic needs. Production expenses accounted for 12.3 percent; emergency cases and medical expenses, 12.29 percent; children's tuition fees, 6.15 percent; and capital for small-scale business, 3.26 percent. Artisanal fishermen largely depended on relatives and friends (43.07 percent) for their credit needs. Those who availed of loans from money lenders paid interest.

In order to appease money lenders or to avoid the doubling of interest, about 5.70 percent rendered menial services and 4.3 percent gave up their domesticated animals as forms of loan payments. About 11.53 percent fell under the category *"bina-bawas sa kita,"* a lending scheme equivalent to cash advance from one's salary. This arrangement is usually resorted to by trawl/basnig workers.

Majority of the artisanal fishermen (74.46 percent) are, thus, caught in the debt-cycle trap. Their earnings from fishing, their primary source of income, is used to partly pay for their debts. Only 16.69 percent pay their debts from money received from their secondary sources of income.

Access to Services

There is no data on a national scale to assess the artisanal fishermen's access to basic social services. However, studies done by the following researchers can provide some insights:

The community study of Leyte fishermen conducted by Roland Q. Jimenez (in Jimenez and Francisco 1984) revealed that service delivery appeared inadequate. Although secondary schools were present in two villages, they had practically no books, supplies and other basic facilities.

Likewise, the health and nutrition services in the villages studied were inadequate. Health workers failed to visit the community on a regular basis. Moreover, information given to households about primary health care and nutrition was insufficient. Jimenez also observed that the children of artisanal fishermen were malnourished.

While the villages had access to a water system, key informants stated that this public utility was far from ideal. Children reportedly became sick due to the unsafe drinking water. Furthermore, many families could not afford to have water piped into their households. Likewise, despite the availability of electricity in the areas covered by the study, majority of the fishing households could not afford the installation fees.

Reportedly, extension workers from the Bureau of Fisheries and Aquatic Resources (BFAR) and other similar government agencies hardly visited them.

LUSSA's (1982) study disclosed that out of 786 respondents, only 16 or 2.03 percent are aware of the Biyayang Dagat Program of the national government. Moreover, although the Biyayang Dagat Program belongs to the ten most-frequently encountered programs, only four percent of the areas studied are implementing the program.

When asked about their problems, identified fishermen respondents in the LUSSA study perceived problems related to feudal and semi-feudal arrangements, foreign intrusion and government programs. Problems affected by the feudal and semi-feudal set up accounted for 82.24 percent of total responses. On the other hand, inadequate government programs and assistance comprised 11.82 percent.

Why are the Artisanal Fishermen Poor?

Smith and others (n.d. as cited by Carner 1981) identified the fishermen's problems and constraints as those related to resources, technology, marketing, and social conditions.

Over-fishing, dynamite fishing, use of fine mesh nets, competition with commercial fishing operations, destruction of coral beds and mangroves, fishpenning and pollution have led to decreased fish resources. Similar problems were identified by Jimenez and Francisco (1984) in their study of the sustenance fishermen in Leyte.

Technological handicaps, meanwhile, include lack of gear and motorized bancas, and high prices of fishing gear and fuel.

Sustenance fishermen also have to contend with marketing problems which include diminishing availability of fish landings, spoilage, lack of transport, price uncertainty, lack of pricing information, and price controls imposed by middlemen. Many fishing villages lack such facilities as a wharf, cold storage, ice plant, fish market, etc.

Unfavorable social conditions include unemployment and underemployment of fishermen, lack of alternative income sources, insufficient potable water, non-ownership of land, theft and damage of gear and poor nutrition. Carner (1981) noted that in relation to nutrition, some families consume a sizeable portion of the catch while others sell all the catch and purchase grains or a lower-grade fish for home consumption.

Carner analyzed the foregoing as mere symptoms of the underlying dependence of fishermen on a common-property, open-access resource (with finite limits of natural production) which is highly perishable once caught, and of the insufficient opportunities for alternative sources of income and food. From evidence that municipal fisheries have already reached, if not exceeded, the maximum sustainable yield, Carner predicted a continuing decline in the average productivity of municipal fishermen.

Conclusion and Recommendations

Artisanal fishermen or marginal fishermen are small-scale traditional fishermen using gears not requiring boats or requiring boats of three tons or less. They fish in both inland and marine coastal waters within three miles of the coastline. There are approximately 600,000 municipal fishermen (100,000 households) located in 10,000 coastal fishing villages throughout the country.

Faced with the problem of declining fish resources, aggravated by the use of low levels of technology and unfair marketing schemes, they supplement their incomes by serving as farm hands or by engaging in trading activities. But even with these, the artisanal fishermen generate an income that can buy only 7.5% of the minimum food requirements for a family of six.

There are various options available for improving the socio-economic conditions of the artisanal fishermen:

1. Provision of capital to enable the artisanal fishermen to own and use motorized bancas and fishing gears. As cited by various researchers, ownership of these productive assets would increase the productivity of the artisanal fishermen as they can fish farther into the sea and better compete with commercial fishing operations. It would likewise increase their income as it would free them from sharing their catch with the owners of these fishing equipment. This option requires access to non-traditional credit sources under socialized credit schemes, since the artisanal fishermen have no collateral, would be considered high risk and, therefore, non-bankable.

2. Organization of artisanal fishermen into political/economic units able to compete with commercial fishing operations, negotiate with middlemen in the marketing of their produce, and undertake the marketing of their produce themselves.

Given that the artisanal fishermen, in general, have no experience in group and cooperative undertaking, as well as in developing their skills in project management, e.g., finance, marketing, setting up and implementation of a management control and information system.

3. Farming does not seem to provide much opportunity. The lowlands, where almost all coastal marine fishing households are located, are characterized by small land fragmentations which are considered too small to be economically viable. Thus, the strategy seems to be that of encouraging backyard gardening and raising of domesticated animals for food self sufficiency, rather than as secondary sources of income.

Other gainful occupations than farming show more promise for increasing income provided the artisanal fishermen are given skills training for alternative employment. These skills training activities should be combined with capital inputs if small-scale entrepreneurial or cooperative enterprises would be implemented. Specific skills training would be more appropriate than general adult education even though the educational level of the population is a limiting factor in alternative employment. Skills training could be focused on immediate viable employment alternatives and would, thus, have a higher and more direct potential for benefits.

A problem arises, however, in either identifying suitable existing work or salary employment opportunities within the household or community. Existing employment opportunities are urban-based. Therefore, unless rural-based industries are created, the benefits of skills training would not remain in the rural areas but would be captured by urban-based enterprises. In addition, the growing labor force and the inability of the economy to provide jobs in the urban areas would make it difficult for the artisanal fishermen to avail of these opportunities.

The above options are, however, pallative in nature. At best, they address problems that are immediate. If, and indeed, the fishing resource is declining due to a continuing depletion/destruction of coral reefs, mangroves, and over-fishing, prospects for the artisanal fishermen to improve their conditions with fishing as the main source of livelihood seem to be dim. Therefore, any development intervention needs to address the problem of declining fish resources as a critical concern. This would require both policy and program review at the national level. Implementation of more stringent measures at the local level for the preservation, conservation and protection of existing fish resource is likewise warranted. Without these measures, there does not seem to be any alternative for the artisanal fishermen in the long-term but to get out of fishing completely and engage in other employment activities. At any rate, alternative does not seem to hold promise unless specific long-term interventions and strategies are implemented in the areas of education and establishment of rural-based industries.

Source: Center for Rural Technology Development

THE SMALL FARM OWNER-CULTIVATORS

Who are the Small Cultivators?

As the name implies, small owner-cultivators own the land they till. They may have bought the land or acquired it through inheritance. As full owners, they exercise complete discretion in matters pertaining to the land and farming (LUSSA 1982).

Ledesma and Cornista (1981) defined the small owner-cultivators as small settlers in a pioneer area usually in the uplands or in the rainfed areas. They are the classical type of peasants who possess their own family farm.

Jimenez and Francisco (1984) subsumed the small owner-cultivators under the broader lowland rainfed farmer category. So called, these farmers depend on rainfall for their sources of water. Their principal produce is rice.

Rivera (1983) assessed that majority of these small growers are direct producers who own their tools of production, land, and who rely mainly on family labor for the production of both their food and cash crops.

Of the studies reviewed, USAID (1980) was the only one which provided some demographic data on paddy farmers. The study noted that paddy farmers suffered from poor nutrition. They could not even afford to eat their own rice throughout the year especially during lean periods. Apparently, farmers prioritized production expenses over their nutritional needs by converting their rice stocks into cash. Their diets suffered until such a time that they have earned enough to buy rice for their own consumption. This pattern was most prevalent among amortizing owners and tenants (Ledesma 1982).

The USAID study also disclosed that household heads of paddy farmer families reached only four to six grades of schooling. Nevertheless, they seemed to be able to send their children to school for a longer period. With an average of four to five children, this prolonged the children's drain on household income but it promised substantial returns to the household in later years.

How Many are They?

Data on this poverty group is sparse and often limited to small areas.

USAID gave a rough estimate of 1.5 million households comprising the lowland rice farmers. The agency arrived at this figure by dividing the lowland rice area of 2.8 million hectares by the average holding of 1.9 hectares.

In the LUSSA study conducted in 1982, the small owner-cultivators constituted the least percentages as compared to share tenants/leaseholders and agricultural workers. In three out of the four crop industries studied by LUSSA, the small owner-cultivators also represented the least number.

In the rice industry, small owner-cultivators rank second to the last in number. The least number is made up Certificate of Land Title (CLT) holders. The small number of owner-cultivators and CLT holders against the bulk of landless workers and tenants led LUSSA to conclude that "the government's efforts to redistribute land through its Land Transfer Program can be hardly called successful or meaningful."

Where are the Small Owner-Cultivators?

According to the USAID study (1980), paddy rice farmers are heavily concentrated in Central Luzon (Nueva Ecija, Bulacan, Pampanga, Tarlac), Western Visayas (Iloilo), Ilocos (Pangasinan), Eastern Visayas (Leyte), Cagayan Valley (Cagayan and Isabela), Bicol (Camarines Sur) and Central Mindanao (Cotabato). These areas are increasingly served by irrigation roads and electricity. Government interest in increasing rice production explains why resources and technology are being channeled to these areas.

How Poor are the Small Owner-Cultivators?

Ownership of Productive Assets

From the studies available, it can be inferred that size of landholdings ranges from one to three hectares. Both LUSSA

(1982) and USAID (1980) observed that farmers tend to subdivide already small plots (of one to three hectares) among sons or sub-lease them among relatives or friends.

World Bank data showed that almost 90 percent of all rice and corn farmers had less than five hectares with the majority (40 percent-corn, and 54 percent-rice) falling within the one to three hectare range. The study found out that 15 percent of the farmers owned farms of less than one hectare.

LUSSA, on the other hand, estimated a much bigger number (76.69 percent) of rice farmers who owned farms of 1/4 to less than two hectares. Only 21.87 percent owned farms of about two to four hectares (Table 24).

Table 24. Size Distribution of Rice Farms, 1982.

CATEGORY	Frequency	%
1/4 to less than 1 hectare	447	42.69
1 hectare to less than 2 hectares	356	34.00
2 hectares to less than 3 hectares	95	9.07
3 hectares to 4 hectares	134	12.80
No response	15	1.43
TOTAL	1,047	99.99

Source: LUSSA Research Staff (1982:215).

A study of the sugar industry revealed a similar pattern. A little less than half of the respondents (49.21 percent) had lands of two hectares and below, while 35.71 percent had farms between 2.25 to four hectares. Unaccounted for were 15.08 percent of farmers who gave no response (LUSSA 1982) (Table 25).

Table 25. Size Distribution of Sugar Farms, 1982.

CATEGORY	Frequency	%
2 hectares and below	62	49.21
2.25 hectares to 4 hectares	45	35.71
No response	19	15.08
TOTAL	126	100.00

Source: LUSSA Research Staff (1982:216).

The same pervasiveness of small farms existed in the coconut industry. As Table 26 shows, 82.36 percent fell within the one to three hectare range. The rest (13.94 percent) had farms measuring between three to seven hectares.

Table 26. Size Distribution of Coconut Farms, 1982.

CATEGORY	Frequency	%
1 hectare to less than 2 hectares	156	30.23
2 hectares to less than 3 hectares	269	52.13
3 hectares to less than 4 hectares	38	7.36
4 hectares to less than 5 hectares	9	1.74
5 hectares to less than 6 hectares	16	3.10
6 hectares and above	9	1.74
No response	19	3.68
TOTAL	516	99.98

LUSSA (1982), USAID (1980) and PPI (1985) agreed that the continuing extensive fragmentation of land severely undermines the productivity of small farmers. The scarcity and the prohibitive cost of land, not to mention the farmers' lack of means to buy land, deter them from availing of more lands to work on, and from improving their income.

Inasmuch as the small owner-cultivator shoulders all the production cost, capital is one of his essential assets. Generally, however, small growers do not contain a cash surplus over and above his family needs. Hence, capital for production is obtained from other sources.

In the case studies conducted by PPI (1985a), data showed that the prevailing average cost of planting for one hectare of rice farm amounts to ₱10,000. Production cost of sugar is even higher (₱11,000), while for coconuts, it is ₱1,000. Apparently, such costs are over and above the earning capacity of the small owner-cultivator who lives on the subsistence level. Hence, the credit cycle begins.

Like the other types of farmers, small owner-cultivators are vulnerable to economic and political forces controlled by big landlords and businessmen. Being direct producers, small owner-cultivators are affected by increases in the prices of manufactured farm inputs such as fertilizers and pesticides as well as other basic commodities (Ibid). For the past two years, for example, prices of fertilizers went up by 120% (PPI 1985).

A cost analysis done by PPI showed that "expenses in production are determined by the monopoly control of the technology and means in agricultural production by foreign corporations." Studies disclosed that local corporations selling fertilizers have pegged prices higher than those of the world market by 27 percent (David and Balisacan 1981 as cited by PPI (1985a).

Aside from capital, small landowner-tillers also own some farm implements. From Aguilar's study, every two or three farmers own rotary weeders, mechanical threshers and carabaos. Moreover, they are able to diversify their household income because of the higher rates of ownership of productive assets as compared to landless rural workers.

In terms of non-productive assets, small owner-cultivators have houses made of permanent and semi-permanent materials. They likewise have access to safe water sources and sanitary toilets.

Small owner-cultivators also own more consumer durables than landless rural workers. In three villages studied, 23 to 45 percent of small owner-tillers owned sewing machines and about half of them had sala sets (Aguilar 1983). Among Ledesma's (1982) respondents, two percent owned refrigerators. In the areas studied by Kikuchi in 1983, 28 percent of small owner-tillers owned refrigerators, while 78 to 86 percent owned radios. In Tubuan, Laguna, 38 percent of the respondents owned bicycles, usually considered as productive income-generating assets.

Income

In relative terms, small owner-cultivators are the least disadvantaged among the rural poor groups. Farmer households with irrigation facilities probably attain average annual incomes very close to the poverty threshold of ₱5,201. For rainfed farmers, average annual income are about 20 percent below the poverty threshold. Paddy farmer households derive a larger share of their income from on-farm employment owing to the higher productivity of their land. In the case of tenants and amortizing land-owners who are covered by Land Reform, the demands of cash-oriented production creates cash flow problems. This results in declining net profit and food consumption. Rice stocks have to be converted to cash in order to meet production expenses. In the process, farmers incur more debts not only for production but also for consumption needs. Several other factors may also cause a decrease in yields, e.g., floods, typhoons, inadequate credit available to purchase petroleum-based inputs, low profitability of recommended fertilizer levels, pest damage and inadequate agronometric practices (USAID 1980).

LUSSA's (1982) findings seemed to place the rice farmers at a level much lower than the poverty threshold. The study noted

82

that majority of rice farmers (leaseholders, share tenants and small owner-cultivators) had incurred deficits or earned nothing at all.

The picture was not as bleak though for the sugar small owner-cultivators. Of the tenants interviewed, 55.86 percent obtained an annual income of ₱3,000 or a daily income of ₱8.00. Majority of the agricultural workers (67.57 percent) earned ₱1,501-₱2,000 a year or roughly ₱4 daily. Small owner-cultivators earned the highest annual income of ₱4,000 or ₱10 to ₱15 a day (Table 27).

For the abaca industry, LUSSA did not specify income according to tenure status. Primary data revealed, however, that 35.85 percent of abaca farmers gained an annual income of ₱1,500-₱2,000 while 30.19 percent earned ₱1,001-₱1,500 a year.

Data for coconut farmers disclosed that most farmers (30.04 percent) earned an annual income of below ₱100 per harvest.(Coconut farmers harvest every 45 days or a maximum of eight times a year.) Others (26.94 percent) earned ₱101-₱200 per harvest. A minority (2.57 percent) earned more than ₱1,000. LUSSA noted that the wage rates in the coconut industry fluctuate according to the market price of copra.

LUSSA concluded that earnings of farmers and farm workers are not enough to meet their basic needs. Citing the Economic Development Foundation (EDF) study in 1976, LUSSA found out that the farmer's annual income of ₱1,500-₱2,000 was way below the minimum income requirement set by EDF. The EDF study estimated that "in 1975, a family of six needed ₱5,020 to be able to live with an adequate diet for a year and must have ₱8,370 in 1976 to be able to live decently. Computed according to the 1980 Consumer Price Index, it becomes ₱12,776.23" (LUSSA 1982).

Marketing of produce which is controlled by both local traders/money lenders and government pricing policy also result in low incomes for the farmers. Aside from exacting usurious

Table 27. Annual Net Income of Tenants, Farm Workers and Small Owner-Cultivators in the Sugar Industry

INCOME	TENANTS		FARMWORKERS		SMALL OWNER-CULTIVATOR		TOTAL LEVEL	
	F	%	F	%	F	%	F	%
than ₱1000	4	3.60	9	4.86	—	—	13	4.18
₱1000-1500	11	9.91	17	9.19	—	—	28	9.00
₱1501-2000	13	11.71	125	67.57	—	—	138	44.37
₱2001-2500	4	3.60	19	10.27	—	—	23	7.40
₱2501-3000	17	15.32	—	—	—	—	17	5.47
₱3001-up	62	55.86	—	—	15	100	77	24.76
No response	—	—	15	8.11	—	—	15	4.82
TOTAL	111	100.00	185	100.00	15	100	311	100.00

Source: LUSSA Research Staff (1982:223).

interest rates, which go as high as 20 to 100 percent, local money lenders/traders further oblige the farmers to sell their produce to them at fixed (usually rock to bottom) prices (PPI 1985b).

PPI also found out that the government's palay support price, which purportedly aims to offset the high cost of production, tend to favor the traders who, in practice, are the ones who establish the original purchase price. Farmers usually have no option but to sell their produce at lower prices because they badly need the cash to pay for their debts. It was observed, too, that the government usually announced the palay support price hikes when the grain is no longer in the farmers' hands. Therefore, the traders still profit in the end.

Moreover, farmers who live at the subsistence level prefer to sell their produce to middlemen at lower prices than to the National Food Authority (NFA). This is largely due to the fact that the NFA can only pay the farmers two weeks after the actual sale. Besides, the agency provides "stringent" requirements as moisture and purity levels. All things being equal, the fact remains that the NFA is capable of buying only 15 percent of the country's palay stocks on the average. At present, NFA keeps an actual palay stock of only nine percent.

Mangahas and others (1976) calculated that owner-cultivafor households in Nueva Ecija earned almost twice as much as lessees and more than twice as much as either tenants or amortizers when income from off-farm sources were included. This difference in income could be attributed to the fact that owners had more remunerative off-farm jobs. Moreover, they were able to accumulate income-generating assets such as poultry, swine, motorized tricycle, and others. The study concluded that income differences across tenures were not significant, whereas those within any particular tenure were relatively large.

Rivera's (1983) study of small owner-cultivators in the banana industry revealed similar results. The small grower received a 22 percent cash share from STANFILCO, the plantation company. From this share, the small landholder still had to deduct his cash advances from the company and pay for the wages of farm workers not directly hired by the company. Rivera also found out that in the Davao area, 97 percent of the small growers had an average credit of ₱7,048 per hectare to STAN-FILCO. The study showed an inverse relationship between credit and size of landholdings. "Growers with less than three hectares have incurred the biggest debts and only those with 26 hectares above, or only one percent of the total hectarage, are out of debt."

Patterns showed that the smaller landholders were being reduced to the status of wage workers. The cash share they got from the company might be equivalent to subsistence wage. This was probably doubly exploitative because the practice of using family labor without due compensation was almost mandatory for the smaller farms heavily in debt to the company.

Although the small landholder still had legal claims over his land, he completely lost control over every phase of the production process for the duration of the contract (usually ten years). In effect, he served himself from his primary means of production — land.

Coping Mechanisms

In order to supplement their meager income, the small owner-cultivators served as tenants in other farms (LUSSA 1982). Some who own carabaos rented them out for an added income of ₱80 a day. Women and children also helped augment the family income by undertaking handicraft production and by working as household help or construction laborers in the city (Jimenez and Francisco 1984). Nonetheless, "additional sources of income do not guarantee income insufficiency or better economic standards for the farmers" (LUSSA 1982). Furthermore employment opportunities available were very limited and a large labor surplus enabled employers to peg wages at substandard levels.

Access to Services and Facilities

The farmers' control of the land provided them access to institutional credit at subsidized interest rates with the possibility of deferred payment (Castillo and Hayami as cited by USAID 1980). There was no institutional credit source available, however, for consumption needs. To cope, farmers turned increasingly to family, friends, neighbors, small rice dealers, millers and the like for short-term loans against the expected harvest (USAID 1980).

In their study, Mangahas et. al. (1976) noted that owners and amortizers relied on government, rural banks, and other institutions for their credit needs. The same study revealed that owners had the largest amounts of outstanding debt followed by amortizers, lessees and share tenants. These data pertain to the crop year 1972-1973 during which Central Luzon suffered from massive flooding. Many indebted farmers failed to make any payment at all during that year. However, the proportion of total defaulters was double among owners and amortizers than among lessees and share-tenants.

A study of lowland rainfed farmers in Leyte revealed that farmers approached middlemen and landlords for their capital needs. The average amount borrowed for every hectare to be planted was ₱500. Farmers paid their debts during harvest time. For every ₱100 borrowed, three sacks of palay were used to pay off the principal as well as its accompanying interest.

The same Leyte study revealed that although services such as electricity, water, education and health were available, these were still inadequate. While two out of four research sites have had access to electric power since 1974, most households could not take advantage of the electric power due to inability to pay.

Sources of drinking water included pumps, open wells and springs. Jetmatic pumps donated by the municipal government in two sites had been out of order for several months. Water obtained from these pumps were musky and foul-smelling such that households could hardly use it.

School facilities in two barangays lacked materials, equipment and teachers. Three of the communities studied completely lacked health services. Thus, they relied on the local *manghihilot* and *arbularyo*. Similar to Lamberte's (1983) findings, one barangay could avail of the services of a doctor and a nurse from the Rural Health Unit mainly due to its proximity to the poblacion. The most common fatal disease was schistosomiasis, followed by pneumonia and malnutrition.

Institutional and infrastructural facilities were likewise inadequate. The barrios lacked milling facilities. Storage facilities did not exist in the barrios. Ordinarily, farmers stored their palays in their houses with hatched roofs that could protect the palay from the rain.

Institutional credit facilities, such as rural banks, were also absent in the areas studied. A few owner-tillers availed of loans from banks in other barrios. Bank officials, however, had difficulty in collecting repayments from these farmers. Extension workers from the appropriate government agencies also rarely visited the areas. At best, projects in only three to five barrios were sufficiently monitored by these technicians.

Conclusion and Recommendations

The preceding discussions offer the following opportunities for increasing productivity and income of the small farm owner-cultivators, as well as for improving their chances for upward mobility.

1. Increasing intensity of land use and crop mix. Given the decreasing farm size and increasing constraints due to continued migration and settlement, intensity of land use and crop mix emerge as important factors influencing the productivity of the small farm owner-cultivator, and, thus, poverty incidence.

   Farming systems can be developed and introduced to the small farm owner-cultivators that address the problems of limited farm size (one to three hectares), increasing costs of farm inputs, vagaries of weather conditions, and lack of access to irrigation facilities. Examples of these farming systems are the KABSAKA and the BUKHAY FARM models developed by the Philippine Business for Social Progress (PBSP).

2. Corollary to the above recommendation is the provision of marketing and technical assistance to the small farm owner-cultivator in identifying marketing opportunities and distribution networks for their produce. Provided adequate research on soil quality and climate conditions viz-a-viz appropriate crop mix are undertaken, cropping patterns can be tailored to what the market demands in specific areas. A good distribution network would enable the farmer to sell his produce in areas where there is a greater demand for his product.

3. Promotion of secondary sources of income. Most of the off-farm activities serve as significant sources of supplementary income for the small farm owner-cultivator. Since land/labor ratio is declining, the share of these activities in rural incomes is likely to increase further. Promotion of these activities will play a significant role in poverty alleviation.

4. Provision of infrastructure support to small farm owner-cultivator. Examples of this infrastructure support are irrigation facilities and farm-to-market-roads, which tend to increase the farmer's land productivity and income.

5. Provision of access to institutional credit services, thus, enabling the small farm owner-cultivator to purchase farm inputs at lower interest rates.

The importance of assisting the small farm owner-cultivator to at least maintain ownership and access to his land cannot be over-emphasized. The existing practice of sub-dividing land for inheritance purposes further decreases the economic viability of the farm. As the land gets smaller, the chances for it to support a household of six become more difficult. With the increasing costs of farm inputs, the small owner-cultivator may resort to the sale of his land to be able to subsist. He, thus, joins the ranks of the landless.

On the other hand, once the small farm owner-cultivator's capacity for increased income is upgraded, he is in a better position to employ farm hands to help him in his farming activities.

COMPARATIVE ANALYSIS OF RURAL POVERTY GROUPS

The description of the groups that are now being referred to as poverty groups highlight the long years of feudalistic tenurial practices and unfair social conditions that cause what has been termed as the culture of poverty. Thus, while the poverty groups may be located in different parts of the country, they inhibit almost the same characteristics and manifest the same behavioral patterns in response to common sets of problems. For the rural poor, the levels of deprivation vary as a consequence of the following:

1) The extent to which they own, control and manage their productive assets, e.g., resource base, production tools;

2) Access to services and facilities (technology, infrastructure support, social services);

3) Extent to which they are gainfully employed;

4) Extent to which they are effectively organized, thus, permitting the group to articulate their needs and mobilize their energies to improve their conditions;

5) The range of opportunities/options available to them.

The urban poor groups is not comparable with the rural poor groups as it aggregates a variety of urban conditions. Also, the dynamics of urban poverty are different.

This section aims to look into the similarities and differences among the rural poverty groups. Owing to a lack of a common definition and measurement standard for determining poverty incidence and levels of deprivation, including the limitations of the micro studies undertaken, the above determinants will be used as basis for comparison purposes. For the urban poor, the weakness of the data base inhibits a meaningful comparison among the groups. Thus, they have been left out in this section.

Extent to Which Poverty Groups Own, Manage, and Control Productive Assets

The landless rural worker neither owns nor possesses tenancy rights to an arable land. Hence, he is totally dependent on the sale of his labor, competing with others for the limited work available in order to survive. Work comes to him in spurts, irregular and intermittent, making him a casual worker in an agrarian setting. The landless rural worker does not own any production tool, hence, his health becomes an important commodity which he sells together with his labor. Having to depend on seasonal employment, he derives an income which can buy only 40% of the minimum food requirements. With no cash surplus and no other sources for daily food consumption, he turns to his employers, relatives, and community friends for loans to buy his daily consumption needs. Payment for these loans are in the form of services. The landless rural worker is, thus, caught in a debt cycle. Not having any control over productive assets, his day-to-day subsistence depends on the availability of employment opportunities as well as on the generosity of his employer.

The upland farmer depends on the uplands and other off-farm employment for his subsistence. He normally owns or has access to a farm size of one to three hectares for which he gets anywhere from 90% to 30% of his total income. Other sources of income include raising of domesticated animals and seasonal employment in the lowlands. Despite these sources, the upland farmer's total income can buy only 65% of the total food requirements for a family of six. Increasing population pressures, the lack of access and non-use of appropriate agriculture and forestry production technologies, and physical inaccessibility limit the productivity of the uplands, therefore, forcing the upland farmer to live below subsistence level. This leaves him with no alternative but to go to the lowlands to seek employment opportunities. This alternative, while giving the upland farmer additional cash source, is still inadequate to support him and his family. He, therefore, like the landless rural worker, turns to his relatives and community for loans to help meet his needs. Unlike the landless rural worker, however, payment for these loans may be in kind or in cash.

The improvement of the socio-economic conditions of the upland farmer, therefore, hinges on the extent to which the uplands are cultivated to a productivity level sufficient to provide food for himself and his family and generate cash surplus to purchase his other needs.

Access to land is not a critical variable for the artisanal fisherman, but rather, the possession of adequate fishing equipment and the problem of declining fish catch. Non-ownership of motorized bancas and fishing gears limits the artisanal fisherman's activities near the shore. He, therefore, cannot compete with commercial fishing operations. Coupled with this problem is the declining fish catch which, if not checked, will make fishing a non-viable proposition as a primary means of livelihood for the artisanal fisherman.

Having access to the sea for food and cash, the artisanal fisherman is not as deprived as the landless rural worker. For the sea, at best, provides him and his family with a source of food for consumption and some cash to buy his other needs. In addition, he raises domesticated animals, engages in informal trading activities, and sells his labor to increase his income. Despite these other sources, the artisanal fisherman's total income is enough only to buy 75% of the minimum food requirements for a family of six.

Provision of credit in easy terms to purchase and own motorized bancas and other fishing equipment, and the implementation of more stringent measures to curb illegal fishing, protect and conserve the fishing resources, seem to be the more

92

critical opportunities to improve the socio-economic conditions of the artisanal fisherman.

The small farm owner-cultivator owns or possesses tenancy right to cultivate a piece of arable land. His farm size ranges from one to three hectares of good land and gives him an income that can purchase 95% of the recommended food requirements for a family of six. His access to land gives the small farm owner-cultivator the opportunity to raise domesticated animals and engage in informal trading activities for additional cash. Having tenancy rights and ownership of the land, he has access to commercial credit sources. It also enables him to join organizations and take advantage of the various opportunities made available to the group. Increasing cost of farm production and further fragmentation of the small farms into uneconomically viable proportions threaten the survival of the small farm owner-cultivator.

Opportunities, therefore, for improving the socio-economic conditions of the small farm owner-cultivator depends on the productivity and the efficiency of farm production. Unless the productivity and viability of the small farms are assured, the small farmer-cultivator may end up joining the ranks of the landless.

Extent of Access to Services and Facilities

Of all the four groups identified, the landless rural worker seems to have the least access to services and facilities. He is followed by the upland farmer and the artisanal fisherman. The small owner-cultivator seems to have the most access to, and the ability to make use of, these resources.

Having no ownership to a productive asset, the landless rural worker cannot avail of loans from institutional credit sources to start or move into other activities to generate income. Having to depend on the sale of his labor, he is too busy searching for employment opportunities to avail of opportunities offered by extension workers, thus, further limiting his options to move into other economic activities. As he depends entirely on the sale of his labor for subsistence, which yield very minimal returns, his children help out and likewise seek employment at the expense of their education.

The upland farmer likewise enjoys very little access to services and facilities. However, because of the importance of the uplands in maintaining balance in the ecosystem, some government programs and projects lately have been implemented in specific areas of the country. Access to roads, market, irrigation facilities, schools, health units and medical personnel continue to be a problem among the upland farmers.

Institutional credit sources are not readily available to the upland farmer. This forces him to turn to his relatives and the community for loans, the payment for which are in kind. The lack of access to marketing opportunities further aggravates the shortage of cash among the upland farmers to purchase his and his family's daily requirements.

On the other hand, the artisanal fisherman does not face the same problems as the landless rural worker and the upland farmer. Being in the lowlands, he has access to schools, health units and the services of extension workers. However, facilities that are critical to the improvement in his income and productivity elude him. Cold storage, fish ports, wharfs and effective marketing organizations are hardly provided, if at all.

The small owner-cultivator has the most access to services and facilities among the rural poor groups. Having ownership and tenancy rights to a piece of land, he uses these as collaterals for obtaining loans. A lot of government efforts have likewise been directed to the small owner-cultivator. Some of these are the Land Reform Program, Rice Sufficiency, Irrigation and Extension Services.

Extent to Which the Groups are Gainfully Employed

The extent to which poverty groups are gainfully employed determines the adequacy — or inadequacy — of incomes derived from their economic activities.

94

Among the groups, the landless rural workers and the upland farmers have the highest seasonal employment. The landless, because he depends on the availability of daily job opportunities; for the upland farmer, his dependence on rain for cultivation. Moreover, these two groups have little possibilities for engaging in other economic activities as they have no access to opportunities that may be available, neither do they have the skill nor the capital to engage in other income-generating activities.

The artisanal fisherman and the small farm owner-cultivator are considered to have moderately seasonal employment since fishing and irrigated farming provide more regular sources of income than cultivating the uplands or working as farm hands. On days when the weather is bad, the artisanal fisherman can engage in farming and other related activities; otherwise, the sea is an open source which at least provides him with food anytime. The small owner-cultivator, on the other hand, especially if his land is irrigated, has the opportunity to engage in year-round farming activities. In addition, he can raise domesticated animals and vegetables for food and cash. He can also engage in informal trading activities, having access to credit and the services of extension workers.

Degree of Effective Organization

The degree to which a group is effectively organized determines, to a large extent, the group's ability to negotiate from a position of power, advantage, or strength.

Of all the poverty groups, it is only the small farm owner-cultivators who are organized on a national scale. This is mainly due to government efforts at organizing them to facilitate the delivery of services. However, the extent to which the small farm owner-cultivator participates in these activities, as well as the effectiveness of these organizations to work for the improvement of the socio-economic status of the small owner-cultivator, have yet to be determined.

Some issues have been brought up with reference to the inability of the groups to organize themselves. For the landless rural worker, it is the fear of repression; for the upland farmer, his inaccessibility and the failure of extension workers to reach him; and for the artisanal fisherman, his having multiple sources of income. In addition, the feeling of helplessness and fatalism that characterize the poverty groups. Whatever the reasons are, the poverty groups have remained unorganized.

Range of Opportunities/Options Available

In essence, the range of opportunities/options available to the poverty groups rests on the extent to which they own, manage, and have access to resources.

The day-to-day search for work inhibits the landless rural worker from moving into other opportunities. The ability to move from one farming area to another encourages the upland farmer to continue his activities in the uplands. He looks for other sources of income only when the upland resources have been depleted. His physical inaccessibility inhibits him from availing of opportunities elsewhere.

The artisanal fisherman, on the other hand, having access to the sea and being located in the lowlands, can engage in a variety of activities that will increase his income. The small farm owner-cultivator can either cultivate his land himself, lease it to another person, or hire farm hands to help him in his activities. Both ways, he has the option to engage in off-farm employment either as a primary source of income or as an income-augmenting activity.

SYNTHESIS AND CONCLUSIONS

From the foregoing comparison of poverty groups, it would seem that the most disadvantaged is the landless rural worker, followed by the upland farmer and the artisanal fisherman. The small farm owner-cultivator is the least disadvantaged of all. The same ranking holds true in terms of possibilities for upward mobility (Table 28).

96

Group	Resource Base/Characteristics	Estimated Households and Incidence of Poverty				Est. Ave. Income as % of 1975 Poverty Threshold	Asset Control	Production Orientation	Employment	Access to Services of facilities	Extent of Organization	Range of opportunities available	Rank in terms of disadvantaged	Upward mobility prospects
		Total Household (000)	No. of % Poor	No. of Poor House- (000)	% to Total Poor									
Landless Rural Worker	Farm Labor o increasingly competitive	600	85	510	13	40	none	Cash or in kind payment for rice, coconut	Highly seasonal	Basically no access	none		1	Low
Upland farmers	Access to virgin forest o forest increasingly becoming limited o soil fertility declines o productivity declining	1500	80	1200	30	60	1-5 hectares of marginal land	subsistence rice and root crops	Highly seasonal	Access limited to specific gov't programs in selected areas	none	limited to upland farming and farm labor	2	Low
Artisanal fishermen	Sea o Fish catch declining	600	80	480	11	75	limited ownership of gear & bancas	Cash for fish	Moderate	o No Community access to inst. level credit o limited access to health, education o limited access to physical and social infrastructures	none	o fishing o farming o trading o farm labor	3	Low
Small Owner Cultivation	Lowland Farms o Fragmentation o Maint. a problem	1590	56	840	21	95	1-3 hectares of good land	Cash rice and other crops	Moderate	o With access to credit, social and physical infrastructure		o farming o trading o entrepreneurial activities	4	Moderate

Sources: Derived from the synthesis of various micro studies.
Calculated from the 1975 Family Income and Expenditures Survey, NCSO.

The landless rural worker, unless given access to a piece of arable land, will remain the poorest of the poor groups in the rural area. For the upland farmer, land security, increasing upland productivity and provisions for secondary sources of income are critical. The artisanal fisherman has to have access to fishing gears and equipment, marketing facilities, and effective organizations to enable him to improve his socio-economic conditions. Moreover, he has to be assured of a continuing fish catch through the implementation of more stringent measures to curb illegal fishing and the destruction of coral reefs.

For the small owner-cultivator, further fragmentation of his farm size should be prevented by increasing farm productivity and providing him with secondary sources of income.

CHAPTER 3
PHILIPPINE URBAN POVERTY

THE URBAN SITUATION

Studies on urban poverty in the Philippines revolve around one setting — the squatter or slum community. Based on a Special Committee Report (as cited in Maslang 1983), squatting is primarily a legal concept which involves the occupancy of a piece of land or building without the permission of the owner. The same report defined slum dwelling as living in homes that are dilapidated and congested such that the condition poses health, fire and crime hazards not only to those who live in the slums but to the whole urban community as well.

Maslang (1983) operationally defined squatting and slum dwelling as two interchangeable phenomena which refer to persons or families who: a) encroach upon private and government properties, such as land, without legal permits; b) live in substandard (dilapidated and congested) dwellings; and c) are generally considered as living below the "poverty line."

A survey on urban poverty studies in the Philippines (conducted by David and Angangco in 1976) revealed that the typical slum dweller is relatively young, usually a migrant, has a meager income, barely possesses an elementary education, is employed in the lowliest occupations and, thus, is both economically and socially exploited.

Notably, rural migrants comprise 80 percent of the slum dweller population. David and Angangco cited four factors which cause this high rate of migration: 1) population pressure upon land resources leading to depletion of natural resources and underemployment in the rural areas; 2) disruption of rural life by war, natural disasters and occasional dissidence; 3) economic opportunities offered by the city; and 4) other opportunities, like better schooling, found in the city.

Castillo (1978) identified the inequality between rural and urban areas and between certain regions in terms of social services, adequacy or lack of development projects and income-earning opportunities as the basic reasons for migration.

Hollnsteiner (as cited in David and Angangco 1976) specified three trends in rural-to-urban migration. The first is the movement to the city of one member of the family, usually the male head, who establishes himself first and then calls for his family. The second trend is where a single child goes to the city and, finding a spouse, eventually stirs up a house in the slum. The third pattern involves the migration of young people called to the city by migrant parents.

The Urban Areas in the Philippines

In 1963, areas classified as urban included those with the following characteristics:

1. In their entirety, all municipal jurisdictions which, whether designated as chartered cities, provincial capitals or not, have a population density of at least 1,000 persons per square kilometer (the whole of Quezon, Baguio and Cebu cities, notwithstanding the minimum density rule are to be included).

2. For all other cities and municipalities with a population density of at least 500 persons per square kilometer, only the poblacion (regardless of population size) plus any barrio having at least 2,500 inhabitants and any barrio contiguous to the poblacion with at least 1,000 inhabitants (for cities where the poblacion is not specified, the central district or the city proper, e.g., for Davao-Bucana (a), Davao Proper (b), and Molave (c), shall be regarded as the poblacion for purposes of this definition).

3. For all other cities and municipalities with a population of at least 200,000 persons, only the poblacion (regardless of population size) and all barrios having at least 2,500 inhabitants, contiguous to the poblacion.

4. All other poblacions having a population of at least 2,500 persons.

Seven years later, in 1970, the definition of urban was changed as follows:

1. In their entirety, all cities and municipalities which have

a population density of at least 1,000 persons per square kilometer.

2. Poblacions or central districts of municipalities and cities which have a population density of at least 500 persons per square kilometer.

3. Poblacions or central districts (not included in 1 and 2) regardless of population size which have the following:

    a) A town hall, church or chapel with religious service at least once a month;

    b) A public plaza, park or cemetery;

    c) A market place or building where trading activities are carried on at least once a week; and

    d) A public building like a school, hospital, puericulture and health center or library.

4. Barrios having at least 1,000 inhabitants which meet the conditions set forth in 3 above, and in which the occupation of the inhabitants is predominantly non-farming/non-fishing.

In their study, Pernia and Paderanza (1980) classified the country's regions into four groups based on the level of urbanization. These are: metropolitan, more urbanized, less urbanized, and rural.

The more urbanized regions include Central Luzon, Southern Luzon, Western Visayas and Central Visayas. Ilocos, Bicol and Eastern Visayas regions represent the less urbanized areas. Meanwhile, the rural areas are Western, Northern and Southern Mindanao.

The authors observed that the Metro Manila area was already at a much higher level of urbanization (77 percent) in 1903 than all the other regions. It then urbanized very rapidly and, by 1970, had completed the entire process. The more urbanized regions of Central-Southern Luzon and Western-Central Visayas, on the other hand, were at a level (10 percent) lower than that of the less-urbanized groups as of 1903. But in 1939, these areas urbanized very rapidly and have reached 30 percent by 1970. Lastly, the less-urbanized regions of Ilocos, Bicol and Eastern Visayas urbanized at a very low pace, gaining

101

only eight percentage points (from 12 to 20 percent) during the entire period from 1903 to 1970. These regions generally suffered from consistently severe net outmigration and have incomes even lower than those in the rural regions. Tables 29 and 30 below illustrate the regional pattern of urbanization for the periods 1903-1970 and 1970-1975, respectively.

Of the country's total population of 48,098 million in 1980, 37.3 percent were residing in the urban areas. Of the total urban population, Metro Manila had the biggest concentration of urban dwellers at 12.32 percent or about 5,925,884 heads. By ranking, Manila was the most urban-populated city at 1,630,000, with Quezon City ranking second with 1,166,000. In terms of density, Manila also registered the highest density at 42,517 persons/km^2; Pasay City ranked second at 20,702 persons/km^2.

In view of the above figures illustrating the dominance of Metro Manila as the urban center of the country, this paper limits its focus on the urban poor of Metro Manila.

Table 29. Regional Urbanization Levels and Tempos,* 1903-1970 (In Percent).

REGION	LEVEL				TEMPO		
	1903	1939	1960	1970	1903-39	1939-60	1960-70
Metropolitan Manila	76.9	90.3	98.1	100.0	3.0	8.3	4.9
More Urbanized	10.1	17.5	26.7	30.5	1.9	2.6	1.9
Central Luzon	11.1	16.5	26.5	31.8	1.3	2.9	2.6
Southern Luzon	10.1	18.0	26.8	32.8	1.9	2.5	2.9
Western Visayas	13.3	21.5	30.5	27.6	1.6	2.2	−1.4
Central Visayas	5.7	13.7	22.2	28.5	2.8	2.8	3.3
Less Urbanized	12.5	16.5	19.8	20.5	0.9	1.0	0.4
Ilocos	13.8	15.9	17.6	20.6	0.5	0.6	1.9
Bicol	14.3	18.0	21.9	21.8	0.7	1.1	− 0.1
Eastern Visayas	9.5	15.4	18.9	19.0	1.6	1.2	0.1
Rural	5.8	16.2	18.6	18.3	3.4	0.8	−0.2
Cagayan	3.4	11.5	14.1	14.3	3.8	1.2	0.1
Western Mindanao	3.8	21.7	16.8	16.2	5.7	−1.6	−0.4
Northern Mindanao	12.5	15.2	20.2	18.7	0.6	1.7	−1.1
Southern Mindanao	1.6	18.1	20.9	21.5	7.8	0.9	0.4
Philippines (excluding Metro Manila)	10.2	12.0	22.9	24.8	1.7	1.8	1.0
PHILIPPINES	13.1	21.6	29.8	32.9	1.7	2.1	1.5

Note: Based on the 1963 urban definition

*Urban-rural growth difference

Source: National Census and Statistics Office. *Census on Population*, various years.

Table 30. Regional Urbanization Levels and Tempos, 1970-75
(In Percent)

REGION	LEVEL		TEMPO
	1970	1975	
Metropolitan Manila	100.0	100.0	4.6
More Urbanized	29.0	30.5	1.5
Central Luzon	30.2	33.9	3.5
Southern Luzon	30.6	31.8	1.1
Western Visayas	26.7	26.7	0.0
Central Visayas	27.9	28.9	1.0
Less Urbanized	19.3	19.5	0.2
Ilocos	19.4	21.1	2.1
Bicol	19.2	18.4	− 0.1
Eastern Visayas	19.4	18.7	− 0.9
Rural	18.9	19.4	0.5
Cagayan	14.1	13.4	− 1.4
Western Mindanao	15.8	14.9	− 1.3
Northern Mindanao	20.9	23.2	2.8
Southern Mindanao	26.6	26.7	0.1
Central Mindanao	15.6	15.5	− 0.2
Philippines (excluding Metro Manila)	23.6	24.5	1.0
PHILIPPINES	31.8	33.4	1.5

Note: Based on the 1970 definition, thus the differences from the 1970 figures of Table 29.

Source: National Census and Statistics Office, 1970 and 1975 censunses Mijares (1984) clarified that urbanization in more developed and less developed countries have different meanings. For the more developed countries, urbanization is synonymous to industrialization and economic growth. In the less developed countries, urban growth is largely the result of rural-to-urban exodus without any major industrial transformation taking place. More often than not, the growth of the urban population has been disproportionately faster than the rural population. This consequently leads to serious social and economic ills such as unemployment, increase of slum areas, housing congestion, and environmental pollution, among others.

URBAN POVERTY IN METRO MANILA

Metro Manila is the country's leading urban center and primate city. To study Metro Manila, therefore, is to study urban Philippines.

Established on November 7, 1975 through P.D. No. 824, Metro Manila consists of four cities and 13 municipalities. These include Caloocan City, Manila, Pasay City, Quezon City, Las Pinas, Makati, Malabon, Mandaluyong, Marikina, Muntinlupa, Navotas, Paranaque, Pasig, Pateros, San Juan, Taguig, and Valenzuela.

A total population of 5,926,000 as of May 1980 occupied Metro Manila's 636 sq. km. land area. With an annual growth rate of about five percent, the city's population reached an 8.2 million mark in 1981 or almost 10 million in 1985. By far, Metro Manila remained as the country's most densely populated region at 12,893 persons per sq. km. as of 1981.

The unabated flow of rural migrants into the metropolis, coupled with a limited economic growth on the national level, resulted in a dramatic rise in slum and squatter colonies in the city. Majority of the squatters are concentrated in Metropolitan cities. Assuming the same rate of increase from 1981 to 1985, it is projected that the most populous Metropolitan cities will be as follows: Manila, Quezon City, and Pasay City.

To provide housing facilities for the growing population, the Ministry of Human Settlements and the National Housing Authority implemented the BLISS, ZIP and PAG-IBIG schemes. Since 1975, however, only 2,307 units have been put up in Metro Manila under these programs. In contrast with Metro Manila's estimated housing backlog of 30,000 units annually and some 180,000 substandard housing units that needed to be improved, the government's housing performance was not substantial enough. NHA itself estimated 415 blighted communities in Metro Manila, excluding Tondo, in urgent need of improvement since 1977. Most occupants of these blighted areas needed to be relocated. Another 123,000 households, occupying 72,500 structures, were in need of upgrading (Ibon Facts and Figures

1981). All in all, the housing problem in Metro Manila is growing in proportion every year.

Income analysis in 1975 showed that 64 percent of the total 770 Metro Manila households earned only ₱7,999 and below. Poverty line in 1975 was pegged by Abrera at ₱7,123. On the basis of these figures, it can be assumed that majority of Metro Manila households live on or below poverty line.

In its survey, NCSO also found that wages and salaries constituted 52.2 percent of the income of Metro Manila households during the second quarter of 1984. This means that employment is the major means of livelihood of a little over half of the city's households. NCSO reported that net receipts from business (22.2 percent) and other sources including pensions (25.6 percent) also provide income.

Majority of the households in the three cities and in the 13 municipalities derived their income from salaries and wages: Caloocan City — 73.5 percent; Pasay City — 61.2 percent; Quezon City — 56.1 percent; and the 13 municipalities — 56.1 percent. Manila, however, only had 39.9 percent, indicating a high unemployment rate.

Nevertheless, NCSO data showed that more than one-third of Manila's households have compensated for the lack of job opportunities by engaging in small-scale businesses such as market and sidewalk vending. This finding was substantiated by 31.6 percent of the households citing net receipts as source of income (DEPTHnews).

THE HAWKERS AND PEDDLERS

Thus far, the most comprehensive study on Manila's hawkers and peddlers was conducted by Sylvia H. Guerrero in 1976. In her study, Guerrero identified three types of hawkers:

1. Mobile-itinerant peddlers and sidewalk vendors who carry their wares around;

2. Semi-static-hawkers in semi-fixed locations — on pavements or sidewalks, by department stores or churches and market areas, with wares often clipped on the walls; and

3. Static-hawkers in more or less permanent locations — in kiosks around market places, sidewalks and vacant lots in commercial areas.

Guerrero was also able to locate the hawkers within Manila by conducting a survey of hawker concentrations within the city. In order to correct for fluctuations in hawker numbers at certain time periods, four enumerations were carried out. These were in the morning and in the afternoon, on a weekday and on a weekend. The survey identified a total population of 4,880 hawker units in Metro Manila. From this number, samples were selected using stratified sampling procedures based on the type of hawker unit location and commodities sold.

These 4,880 hawker units could be broken down further into three types of hawkers: 545 mobile, 4,004 semi-static and 331 static. Classified by type of commodity, the survey results are as follows: unprocessed food sellers numbered 1,733 followed by sellers of non-food, non-durable items numbering 1,326. The counts for other sellers are: processed food, 228; prepared food, 737; textile and clothing, 338; service, 306 and unclassified items, 141.

The study also reveals that the Manila vendor comes from the low-income, congested shanty towns of the metropolis. Two out of three vendors are female, 30 years or younger, has had an elementary or some high school education, and has lived in the city for over a decade, if not a native of the city. She comes from a large family and the earnings from her peddling helps augment the family income.

A typical peddler conducts most of her daily business in an area of one sq. m. or less, in the mornings around market areas or in the afternoons and evenings in the business districts and in transportation nodes of the city, like Quiapo. Daily earnings amounted to P5-P10 at the time of the study. Her business is small, employing no assistants or relatives. She obtains her goods on a cash-and-carry basis or on consignment.

Guerrero estimated an 80 percent probability that a vendor has no license and is, thus, subject to apprehension by law enforcement agents. Like the scavengers, the government also formulated policies to regulate, if not totally eradicate, peddling. The reasons for prohibiting peddlers in certain areas of Metro Manila include: 1) sidewalk vendors obstruct pedestrian and vehicular traffic; and 2) sidewalk and street vendors do not pay fees and, therefore, offer unfair competition to regular stall holders who pay fees and carry licenses. Despite continued arrests and confiscation of goods, however, peddlers and hawkers still persist and continue to operate.

Guerrero asserted that the hawker problem will continue to receive limited or unrealistic treatment if one were to consider it simply as either a law enforcement problem or a public health liability. Interviews showed that 19 out of 25 officials opined that a legal and punitive approach in solving the hawker problem has had limited success, notwithstanding the persistent efforts on the part of Manila law enforcement agencies.

Guerrero also observed that the highest hawker density in Manila's central business districts coincides with peak commuters' traffic, when lower and middle income wage earners and students wait for their rides home during the late afternoon and early evening hours. Thus, she suggested to integrate the buying activities of the purchasing and commuting public and the hawking activities of peddlers and vendors by designating areas where peddlers may sell and the public may buy during specified hours.

108

She also suggested that a bureau or office, which can formulate and implement policies which are more supportive of the needs of the hawkers, be established. This office may take charge of problems of licensing and fees, the formation of cooperatives, financing and marketing assistance. Tie-ups with small-scale or cottage industries can be established by such an office so that vendors can serve as legitimate agents of small-scale industries. This way, hawking and peddling may be viewed as a trade that can develop prospective entrepreneurs rather than as a "refuge occupation."

Moreover, Guerrero proposed that younger hawkers may be trained in order to provide them with skills to enable them to gain employment in industrial or business concerns. For the older ones, more structural solutions, such as increasing their opportunities to engage in small-scale business by providing small loans and organizing them into cooperatives, might prove more realistic.

Finally, she recommended that stalls with sanitation facilities be constructed in certain areas of the city. Such stalls can be utilized by the vendors at minimal fees. This scheme will improve the image of the hawkers and eventually expand their clientele.

Conclusion and Recommendations

The hawkers and peddlers present themselves as one distinct poverty group in Metro Manila in dire need of development assistance from government as well as private agencies. To date, they are a neglected group and worse, government's attitude towards them is such that in order to solve the problem, the whole business of peddling must be regulated, if not totally eradicated. Such prohibitive policy is not at all supportive of the poverty group's aspiration for a better life.

Basically, Guerrero, in her study, pointed out that a peddler's major problem in his activity is how to realize his status so that he avoids the nuisance of being apprehended by police authorities that, from time to time, hampers the conduct of his trade.

Prevailing government policies prohibit peddling in certain districts of the city and require peddlers to obtain due licenses to enable them to freely conduct their trade. Other problem areas include financing and procurement of goods.

Faced with this situation, a peddler, if he decides to stick it out with his trade, is confronted with several options, as follows:

1. Maintain his "illegal" status and evade apprehending law enforcers during raids in which case, he appear to be sanctioned by paying necessary fines and/or be arrested;

2. Legalize his trade by complying with city ordinances and policies;

3. Band together with fellow peddlers to form an association with the capacity to negotiate and deal with government, as well as private agencies, to advocate for favorable policies/programs and undertake socio-economic projects to promote their own welfare.

The peddling problems present an opportunity area for development agencies to be involved in alleviating the plight of the peddlers. These opportunity areas can be spelled out as follows:

Government

1. Premised on the assumption that peddling is closely intertwined with the squatting and urban congestion problem, the government may adopt, as a major policy, the stance of discouraging urban migrants by creating alternative employment sites in urban peripheries and rural areas, similar to an "industry dispersal' or "back-to-the-province" program. This is proposed to be a long-term and comprehensive solution to address the complex problem of squatting-peddling.

2. Guerrero pointed out that one strategy is to establish a government bureau or office that can formulate and

enforce policies and programs that answer the particular problems of the peddlers, as follows:

a. Reasonable licensing requirements and fees;

b. Designating specific sites for peddlers where they are allowed to ply their trade freely;

c. Formation of credit and probably housing cooperatives;

d. Linkaging the peddlers' group with existing resource agencies.

Private Voluntary Organizations

PVOs can also complement government efforts through intervention strategies such as:

1. Provision of organizational and group-building inputs to peddlers as a collective entity so that an association is formed with advocacy and project management capabilities to work for their collective good;

2. Provision of socialized credit financing to organized peddlers;

3. Implementation of low-cost housing programs and services to address the attendant problem of squatting/urban congestion;

4. Implementation of other basic services that answer the needs of the peddlers.

THE SCAVENGERS

In 1982, William Keyes conducted a study on what can be considered as the lowliest and least regarded of the urban poor — the scavengers. His study, however, was limited only to the scavengers in Maligamgam, Sampaloc, Manila.

Keyes' study revealed that the scavengers are a heterogenous group. Sixty percent of those studied were born in Manila but are sons of migrants. More than half are male, married and with children, and in their mid-twenties. Women family breadwinners scavenge on their own. Boys as young as eight also scavenge, usually in groups of two or three. Other families go out together.

Respondents included in the study have been scavenging for five years. All of them see scavenging as the only means to earn a living, although given a choice, interviewees prefer other occupations to scavenging. Most respondents have never held permanent salaried jobs; some were once construction workers or government casuals.

Scavenging is a six- to seven-day-a-week job for most of the adults. Normally, carts go out in the early morning returning at about 10:00 a.m., and then leave again at about 6:00 p.m. turning in around midnight. The sun's heat along with patterns of garbage disposal make mid-day scavenging unattractive and unprofitable. Unless borrowed by younger scavengers, the carts usually lie idle at mid-day.

In the course of the study, a government anti-scavenging drive resulted in the impounding and burning of carts.Scavengers had to take turns using whatever carts remained. This considerably curtailed operations.

On income, half of the respondents reported to have earned P3.00 a day. However, the modal range appeared to be P4.00 to P6.00. Factors influencing income were: access to a *suki* (regular source of scrap materials), good fortune, physical stamina, and availability of carts.

Several factors also make life more difficult for the scavengers. These are restrictive government policies, competition at the source and price structures within the system.

Keyes identified three forms of government harassment of the scavengers and the poor, in general. On June 14, 1974, the city government passed Ordinance No. 7510 prohibiting scavenging and providing penalty for violation thereof. Scavenger carts were impounded and burned; *bodegas* were dismantled by the City Engineer's Office, and scavengers were arrested, fined and detained. The scarcity of carts forced families to share the few remaining ones so that family earnings dropped even further below subsistence levels. Left without other opportunities, scavengers continued to work at their trade despite the ban, but now with greater risk and lower earnings.

A second area of government harassment emerges from the fact that scavengers are also usually squatters. At the time of the research, government anti-squatter resettlement programs were being vigorously pursued and large numbers of urban squatters, scavengers among them, were being relocated in distant places outside of the metropolitan area. This resulted in a significant drop of family earnings after the enforced transfer. Being now far removed from places of employment, a minimum wage earner even had to spend a greater part of his salary for transportation. Furthermore, while proximity to the diversity of urban life offered a variety of secondary income opportunities for the family, relocation to a remote site where everyone is poor has virtually extinguished their opportunities.

A third area of government harassment is the persistence of the *lagay* system. Scavengers pursuing an illegal occupation are easy prey for unscrupulous policemen. Maligamgam's poor remains victims of extortion despite official government efforts to curb such practices.

Another problem confronting the scavenger is the limited access to the "real wealth" available from scrap materials. In an economic situation where the multitude are poor, where family income must be stretched, and business competition is keen, very little valuable scrap material trickles down to the scavenger. About 70 percent of what the scavenger collects are classified as "waste no. 2", the lowest grade of scrap for which he receives only P0.07 kilo. Needless to say, the scavengers have a poor bargaining position in pricing the scrap materials. The cartload of waste materials first goes to the *bodegero* then to the dealer and, finally, to the factory with a corresponding mark-up at each level.

Keyes also noted the "competition" between the scavengers and the "garbage men" employed by the government. While collecting, garbage men also sort out paper, plastic and metal, and delay their collecting to bring these items for direct sale to the *bodega*. Despite this practice, there does not seem to be any open hostility between scavengers and garbage men.

Keyes expressed three main recommendations on social, government and business policies in relation to the poor.

On social policy, Keyes asserted that the public, especially those who yield political and economic power, needs to become more keenly aware of the limited opportunities open to the poor and the hardships they must face everyday. Accordingly, they must consider giving higher priority to the welfare of the poor in policy-making and administrative decisions. In effect, this requires a long-range conscious attempt to change society's attitudes towards the poor.

Keyes also suggested that government policy towards scavengers should generally be one of non-interference or toleration, not suppression until viable alternatives for economic opportunity can be made available. In the face of wide-scale unemployment, the government should be ready to support and encourage people who have found even marginal gainful employment.

Finally, Keyes called on the paper industry to recognize the necessity of backward integration in order to rationalize the entire chain of activities in the system. This means a backward integration that openly accepts social costs which cannot be justified in terms of return on investment, a backward integration that rationalizes present *bodega* and dealer procedures

115

and which, at the same time, rejects capital intensive "antiseptic" and automated solutions in a labor-intensive environment.

The research results suggested that manufacturers must realize that, up to the present, they have not been paying the costs; that by limiting their horizons to one link in the chain, they have allowed a pattern of dehumanizing exploitation. *Bodegeros* and dealers are generally not educated business leaders with a sensitivity to basic economic concerns. It is on the corporate level, where talented and hopefully enlightened leadership is more likely to be available, that solutions must be worked out. Through enlightened leadership, supported by wise goverment policy, business must begin to accept the social costs of the industry within which they have been operating.

Conclusion and Recommendations

Keyes' study indicated that scavenging is the lowliest occupation of the urban poor. This situation makes the scavengers' plight even worse than the peddlers'/hawkers' group.

The scavengers group, like the peddlers and hawkers, experience government harassment in several ways. The government's policy of anti-scavenging does not help any of these poverty groups. Worse, it further complicates the already tight situation the scavengers find themselves in.

From the viewpoint of development agencies, the scavenging issue presents an opportunity area to extend development assistance to this poverty sector. As a matter of possibilities on how to address the scavenging problem to benefit most the scavengers' sector, the following options (for development agencies) are presented as initial take-off points:

1. For government to adopt a policy of toleration rather than prohibition in support of scavenging as an activity;

2. Creation of a government office to look after the welfare and interest of the scavengers as a distinct poverty group, most probably in line with employment genera-

tion and ecological balance/health and sanitation programs;

3. For private business enterprises to identify a useful role for scavenging in the whole process of recycling waste materials for industrial and other consumption;

4. For scavengers to be organized into cooperative associations/groups that are able to negotiate and bargain with middlemen/dealers/factory owners so that they get a **fair share of the cash returns of the trade;**

5. For funding agencies involved in socialized credit to extend credit assistance to organized scavengers' groups so that collectively, they can put up a "cartel" and do away with unscrupulous middlemen in the process;

6. Finally, for enterprising scavengers' groups to be provided with technical training to engage in some scrap/waste recycling-related projects to enable them to expand their operations.

These recommendations are based on the premise that scavenging, as a source of livelihood for the marginal poor, is here to stay in our society and unless the whole problem is addressed to at its "roots" (that is, lack of more decent employment opportunities in the economy), then the government will have to contend with the scavenging problem for the time being. However, both short-term and long-term solutions will have to be worked out to address the problem.

THE URBAN LABORERS

As mentioned earlier, a little over half of Metro Manila households (52.2 percent) derived income from employment in the second quarter of 1984. Based on David and Angangco's study, roughly 50 percent or more of the urban poor were skilled workers such as drivers, plumbers, electricians, painters, or carpenters. A very small proportion were white-collar workers such as managers, small proprietors, and sales and clerical workers. A bigger proportion consisted of unskilled laborers engaged in such jobs as being pier hands, janitors, "peons", factory casuals, and the like.

These jobs do not offer high pay; slum dwellers are also faced with a more pressing problem of security of tenure. The NCSO data of 1981 showed that the National Capital Region (Metro Manila) exhibited the lowest labor force participation rate both in the fourth quarter of 1980 (53.4 percent) and in the fourth quarter of 1981 (53.1 percent). This was largely due to the closure of factories and private companies (Maslang 1983). Unemployment rate in 1979, at 6.5 percent, rose to 14.6 percent in 1980. Out of 49,036 lay-offs recorded nationwide from January to September 1980, 30,860 were in Metro Manila (Business Day, May 1981 as cited in IBON Facts and Figures, June 1981). Wage and salary earners who formed majority of the employed population and the majority of the lowest income group had an average yearly income of P5,640. Moreover, their incomes are static and declining in terms of purchasing power (IBON Facts and Figures, June 1981).

Conclusion and Recommendations

The current government policy to attract huge foreign capital to flow into our country has created much toll to thousands of Filipino urban laborers. This economic package which includes, among others, cheap wages, an emasculated labor force

119

and generally lower cost of production has caused the present dispensation to disintegrate into a backward capitalist economy, highly dependent on advanced nations for investments, technology, markets and loans. In the long run, the poor Filipino laborers suffer the brunt of industrial fluctuations like lay-offs, depressed wages and factory closures.

Such a problem may be rooted out and solved with a comprehensive and genuine industrialization program that will look first and foremost into the welfare of the poor Filipino laborers. The government, hand-in-hand with the private development institutions, can work together towards this end.

Government

Programs and policies must be geared towards:

1. Encouraging/Promoting/Assisting local small- and medium-scale industries not only in urban centers but also in the remote countrysides;

2. Dismantling the monopoly control over human and natural resources, ensuring instead the poor Filipinos to have greater access to these resources;

3. Encouraging more harmonious labor-management relationship;

4. Encouraging the organization of genuine and independent labor unions that have the capacity to protect and assert their own interests;

5. Decentralization of economic activities towards developing industrial growth areas in other regions.

Private Development Organizations

1. Development of programs/technologies that will benefit the labor sector, such as livelihood and organizational skills development;

2. Initiating regular consultation activities with labor sectors to serve as fora in ventillating labor-management issues and concerns.

120

GENERAL RECOMMENDATIONS/ISSUES AND CONCERNS

Any task of providing development assistance to urban poverty groups will have to consider the peculiar dynamics of urban poverty as distinguished, for instance, from rural poverty. The following are some proposed areas for consideration to development policy-makers and managers:

1. The complex problem of urban poverty will have to be addressed to in an integrated manner such that programs and services are designed to answer not only the economic aspect but other equally important areas such as housing, health and nutrition, access to credit resources, education and even the need to organize the urban poor for a strong negotiating position with government and private agencies;

2. Development agencies must be prepared to allocate substantial investments/resources in implementing urban poor development programs. For instance, a socialized credit program would require high-risk exposure of funds to urban poor groups on a subsidized scheme;

3. Non-traditional sources of financing for urban poor groups such as cooperatives, mutual help associations and other indigenous structures must be developed as alternative sources of credit to support the poor's economic activities;

4. Programs for the urban poor may call for more innovative and replicable project schemes to ensure effectiveness and maximum benefits for the beneficiary groups; and

5. Further research studies must be conducted on the urban poverty situation to provide reliable and accurate data base for development policy-makers/planners/managers.

EPILOGUE

DEVELOPMENT ASSISTANCE STRATEGIES AND APPROACHES

Various organizations in the Philippines, government and non-government alike, have continued to undertake efforts addressed at curbing the problem of poverty. Together with such efforts, though, forces that obstruct the transformation process (i.e., feudalistic, societal structures and others) have made the problem much more complex. But there is no turning back in the struggle to crack the shell of the poverty trap. Results of past efforts should be used as springboard for future endeavors.

Whatever economic growth the Philippines has experienced over the past years has been of little benefit to the majority of the Filipino poor. The common set of problems and the issues brought forth in the analyses emphasize the need for development goals to include not only economic growth but likewise the reduction in income disparities and eradication of poverty.

The updated Philippine Development Plan for 1984-1987, unlike the previous ones, speak of principal targets — the farmers, fishermen, fixed-income earners, and other low-income groups. The goals for these groups and the country as a whole include increased productivity for "sustained economic growth, more equitable distribution of the fruits of development, and total human development. The plan, among others incorporates implementation of programs addressed towards minimizing inequality in the distribution of income, low productivity, imbalance in the distribution of, and access to services, facilities and investments among regions, unemployment and underemployment and high population growth rates. This shift to a more targetted approach reflects the government's realization that prior development efforts had been "relatively ineffective in reaching the masses of poor people and that there is a widening gap between the rich and the poor." Thus, growth and equity considerations must go together in national development planning and administration.

Marcus D. Ingle (1982) traced the evolution of Development Assistance Policies and Strategies over the years 1950-1970. He categorized the approaches into untargetted strategies, semi-targetted and targetted strategies/approaches, as manifested in three major periods:

The first phase, in the 1950's and early 1960's, sought maximum growth in the economies of developing nations and assumed that trickle down and spread effects would incorporate the majority of the poor into productive economic activities. The policies sought rapid and high rates of growth in national output with little concern for distributive effects. The development policies of the 1950's sought to overcome obstacles and eliminate the bottlenecks to economic growth through social change by "redistributing productive assets, developing human resources, controlling population growth and increasing productive capacity in various sectors of the economy." Sectoral programs were aimed at affecting large numbers of people whose social or economic characteristics were considered to be obstacles to development. Technical and financial assistance were more focused and concentrated on specific development programs and on groups of people with characteristics thought to be adverse to economic growth.

The policies of the 1970's sought economic growth with social equity and were concerned as much with the distribution of benefits as with the rate and pace of economic output. They sought to "channel, to the poor majority, resources to subsistence population in rural areas, provide for basic human needs in the poorest areas, and improve the economic and living standards of the poor." These objectives were to be pursued through targetted assistance strategy (Table 31).

THE USAID EXPERIENCE

The United States Agency for International Development (USAID), among the large international donor agencies, has, perhaps, the widest experience in providing assistance to developing countries. Its development aid policy have gone through all the three phases as outlined by Ingle. Under the U.S. Foreign Assistance Act of 1973, the American Congress declared that "American aid would depend less on large-scale capital infrastructure and industrial expansion" but would focus on "alleviating problems of the poor majority in developing countries." Moreover, that U.S. development efforts must be able to demonstrate "positive effects on the well-being of the poor and that the relative position of the poor vis-a-vis the wealthy within any given country should be maintained and improved as a consequence of development assistance."

An analysis of USAID's experience with several targetted or poverty-focused projects revealed certain generic management characteristics evident in successful and absent in unsuccessful projects. These characteristics are as follows:

* Clearly stated poverty-reduction objectives:

* Clearly identified groups and subgroups constituting the poor;

* Clearly identified causes of poverty for groups and subgroups;

* Clearly specified sets of distribution mechanisms for assuring that benefits accrue to intended groups;

* Clearly specified institutional arrangements to operate distribution mechanisms; and

* Clearly specified feedback and assessment system oriented to poverty-reduction objectives.

IMPLEMENTING POVERTY-FOCUSED PROGRAMS AND PROJECTS

While it might seem easy to implement targetted or poverty-focused programs and projects, certain implications have to be considered at the policy and management (policy execution) levels.

A. Policy Level

   1. Any development agency, or for that matter, the government, must first adopt employment and equity as development goals which are of equal importance as economic growth.

   2. A commitment to bottom-up planning rather than the present top-to-bottom centralized planning process. Concomittant with this is the commitment to develop self-reliance among community and grassroots organizations (poverty groups) and enable them to participate in planning, decision-making and implementation of programs and projects affecting their lives.

   3. Willingness to invest, allocate, and channel resources in favor of the poor. This includes financial, technical and manpower resources.

   4. Willingness to decentralize administration of programs and projects, if necessary. This might mean a redefinition of central office roles and giving up certain powers and authority in favor of its branches or sub-groups.

B. Management Level (Policy Execution Process)

   The success factors, as mentioned by Ingle, manifest themselves in the following phases of the policy execution process: strategy formulation, project design, project implementation and benefit continuation (Table 32).

   Inherent in the model is the development and implementation of an effective monitoring and evaluation scheme that will both measure progress of program implementation as well as its impact at the beneficiary level.

Table 31. Comparative Overview of Major Development Policies and Aid Strategies.

CHARAC-TERISTICS	DEVELOPMENT POLICIES		
	Growth Maximization with Trickle-Down of Benefits	Economic Growth Sectoral Development Growth Policies	Economic Growth with Social Equity Policies
A. STRATEGY W/ REGARD TO THE POOR	Untargetted	Semi-targetted	Targetted
B. POLICY OBJECTIVES 1. Overall goals	o Promote high and sustained rate of economic growth through capital-intensive industrialization.	o Promote high and sustained rate of economic growth by overcoming bottle-necks and obstacles to development in key sectors.	o Achieve rates of economic growth consistent with widespread participation in economic activities and equitable distribution of benefits
2. Specific goals	o Increase GNP and create surplus imbalance of International payments. o Increase real per capital incomes and demand for consumption and capital goods o Stimulate savings, capital formation and investment in export production and import substitution industries.	o Increase productivity in key sectors-agriculture commercial services, etc. o Increase real per capita income and internal demands for domestically produced goods and services. o Increase levels of health, education, nutrition. o Lower population growth rates	o Increase productivity and income of those living in absolute or relative poverty. o Reduce disparities in income and wealth o Redistribute income and wealth o Satisfy basic human needs o Assure full employment o Promote economic self-reliance
3. Types of Benefits	o Economic, national output, highly aggregated	o Economic and social; sectoral output; moderately disaggregated	o Economic and social; productivity and income; disaggregate to household level
C. INTENDED BENEFICIARIES 1. Coverage	o Society as a whole; capital investors and workers most directly	o Occupation groups within key sectors and capital investors and workers in related sectors	o Groups and individuals considered relatively or absolutely poor
2. Sequence of Benefit Distribution	o Capital investors and employees of industrial sectors — benefits "trickle down" to agricultural workers, tertiary industry workers, public sectors and others	o Capital investors and workers in key industries; benefits will spread to other sectors as national economy grows	o Relative and absolute poor, with aggregation of benefits to these groups contribution to national development
D. NATURE OF THE INTERVENTION 1. Characteristics	o Poverty group neither identified nor singled out for specific attention during the course of implementation	o Poverty group identified but not singled out for attention during implementation	o Poverty groups identified with a broad range of characteristics, e.g., health, education, income, race, religion, sex, etc. o Specific characteristics of the poverty groups targeted for improvement, i.e., level of income, level of malnutrition, etc. singled out during implementation

CHARAC-TERISTICS	Growth Maximization with Trickle-Down of Benefits	Sectoral Development Growth Policies	Economic Growth with Equity Policies Equity Policies
2. Policy Rationale	o Single market mechanisms are at work in the economy which automatically distribute benefits in an equitable manner, then only minimal intervention in the market process is required	o Since market mechanisms are not working properly then sectoral interventions are required to correct the imbalances in the market system	o Since large segments of the poor are excluded from the development process even when market mechanisms are functioning properly, then other non-market interventions must be supported.
3. Methods of Policy Intervention	o Heavy reliance on private sector organizations and market mechanisms, with government providing policy incentives, social overhead investments, and proper "environment" for entrepreneurship and capital formation	o Heavy public sector investment in social overhead and directly productive activities in key sectors o Creation of conditions conducive to private investment in key sectors o Active government role in providing social services needed to overcome bottlenecks to development	o Public policies, programs and projects tailored to needs of the poor o Reliance on broad range of institutions including government bureaucracies voluntary organizations, private enterprise, local authorities, and special interest groups to deliver services and organize the participation of the poor
4. Distribution Mechanisms	o Market mechanisms will operate automatically to generate growth and distribute benefits through "trickle down" process	o Primarily market mechanisms with government intervention to ensure wider distribution and stimulate growth in lagging sectors and regions.	o Strong government intervention through programs and projects tailored to the conditions and needs of constituent groups of the poor
E. PRIMARY INDICATORS OF DEVELOPMENT	o Level of GNP o Increase in Per capita GNP o Employment in Industry o Rate of Capital Formation o Rate of Gross Domestic Investment o Rate of Internal Savings o Productivity of Labor o Levels of Consumption	o Level of Per Capita GNP o Contribution of Primary, Secondary, and Tertiary Sectors to GNP o Rate of Growth in Output of Key Sectors o Percentage of Labor Force Employed o Structure of Land Distribution o Other Economic Growth Indicators o Population Growth Rates	o Structure of Income and Wealth Distribution o Life Expectancy o Death, Birth, and Morbidity Rates o Literacy Rates and School Enrollments o Nutritional Levels o Ratios of Health Facilities to Population o Condition of Housing Stock

Source: Marcus D. Ingle. "Reaching the Poor Through Development Assistance: An Overview of Strategies and Techniques." Paper presented at the American Society for Public Administration Annual Meeting. Honolulu, Hawaii Hawaii, March 21-25, 1982.

Table 32. Management Characteristics in Consecutive Phases of Successful Growth with Equity Policy Execution Process.

GENERAL CHARACTERISTICS	MANAGEMENT CHARACTERISTICS AT EACH POLICY EXECUTION PHASE			
	STRATEGY FORMULATION	PROJECT DESIGN	PROJECT IMPLEMENTATION	BENEFIT CONTINUATION
1. Clearly stated poverty reduction objectives.	Overall poverty reduction objectives should be established and clearly stated by major development participants	Specific poverty reduction objectives should be clearly stated and agreed upon by major project participants.		
2. Identification of groups and sub-groups constituting the poor.	Various groups constituting the poor should be identified	Sub-groups constituting the poor in the project area should be identified and described.		
3. Identification of causes of poverty for groups and sub-groups.	Causes of poverty for each group should be identified.	For each project-specific group and sub-group constituting the poor, the causes of poverty should be described and analyzed.		
4. Specification of which types of benefits are to accrue to which groups and sub-groups.	Intervention strategies should identify which groups are to benefit. In selecting or priorizing groups, the model developed by Kepner and Trego can be used. Seriousness of the problem urgency, growth potential and impact.	The proportion and sequencing of benefits which are expected to accrue to intended beneficiaries should be clearly stated.	Project implementors should agree on who intended beneficiaries are, where they are located, and what benefits are supposed to accrue to them overtime.	
5. Specifications of the necessary set of distribution mechanisms for assuring that benefits accrue to intended groups.	The strategy should indicate the general types of distribution mechanisms that are available and will be given priority.	The project intervention should specify the necessary set of distribution mechanisms for assuring project benefits accrue to intended groups.	For each unique beneficiary group or sub-group, project interventions should include the necessary of distribution mechanisms to assure that	For each beneficiary group, the necessary distribution mechanisms should be used to continue the flow of benefits.
6. Specifications of the types of institutional arrangements to operate distribution mechanisms.	The strategy should describe suitable institutional arrangements for implementing the poverty reduction policy.	The project design should specify the institutional arrangements to be used in operating distribution mechanisms.	Institutional arrangements for properly operating distribution mechanisms.	Institutional arrangements to operate distribution mechanisms should function properly.
7. Specifications of a feedback and assessment system oriented to poverty reduction objectives.		The project intervention should provide for a feedback and evaluation system to monitor the achievement of poverty reduction objectives.	A feedback and evaluation system should be in use to assess achievement of poverty reduction objectives and to allow adaptation of the project to changing conditions.	A feedback and evaluation system should be in place to allow institutional actors to adapt resource inputs to the achievement of long-term poverty reduction objectives.

BIBLIOGRAPHY

AGUILAR, Filomeno V. Jr. Landlessness and Hired Labor in Philippine Rice Farms.

ARDALES, Vinancia and Felly David. The Poverty Condition of Artisanal Fishermen in Iloilo Province.

BAUTISTA, Gemelino. "Socio-Economic Conditions of the Landless Rice Workers in the Philippines: The Landless of Sta. Lucia as a Case in Point".

_____ , William C. Thiesenhusan and David King. "Farm Households on Rice and Sugar Lands: Margen's Village Economy in Transition".

BERNALES, Benjamin C. and Angelita P. de la Vega. Case Study of Antique Development Program.

BOGLOSA, Reinerio D. "Concentration of Landholdings and Rural Poverty in Western Visayas 1970-1971".

CARNER, George. "Survival, Interdependence and Competition Among the Philippine Rural Poor".

DOZINA, G. E. and G. W. Herdt. Upland Rice Farming in the Philippines.

DULDULAD, Anaclet C. "The Kaingeros as Focus of Development".

Forum for Rural Concerns. Negros: A Primer on the Sugarland Crisis.

GANAPIN, Delfin J. Factors of Underdevelopment in Kaingin Communities Laguna.

GONZAGA, Violeta L. Mechanization and Labor Employment: A Study of the Sugarland Workers' Response to Technological Change in Sugar Farming in Negros.

INGLE, Marcus D. Reaching the Poor Through Development Assistance: An Overview of Strategies and Techniques.

In Search of the Assetless Poor.

JACKSON, Dudley. Poverty.

JIMENEZ, Pilar R. and Josefa S. Francisco. The Rural Poor in Leyte: A Social and Institutional Profile.

KERVILET, Benedict J. Profiles of Agrarian Reform in a Nueva Ecija Village.

KIKUCHI, Masao. "Recent Changes in a Laguna Rice Village: A New Generation of Changes".

LAMBERTE, Exaltation Eloevira. "Macro-level Indicator of Upland Poverty: The Case of the Delivery of, and Access to, Services in Upland Areas".

Landless Workers and Rice Farmers: Peasna Sub-classes under Agrarian Reform in Two Philippine Villages.

LEDESMA, Antonio J. "A Typology of Filipino Peasant in the 1980s.

Luzon Secretariat for Social Action Research Staff. Countryside Report Focus on Five Major Industries: Rice, Coconut, Sugar, Abaca and Fishing.

LYNCH, Owen J. A Survey of Research on Upland Tenure and Development.

MAKIL, Lorna R. and Patricia N. Fermin. Landless and Other Rural Workers in the Philippines: A Documentary Survey.

MANGAHAS, Mahar K. "Measuring Poverty and Equity Through Perception Variables".

        , ed. Measuring Philippine Development.

        , Virginia A. Miralao and Roman P. de los Reyes. Tenants, Lessees, Owners: Welfare Implications for Tenure Change.

National Economic and Development Authority. Social Development: The Philippine Approach.

National Situations: Social Science Sector.

Updated Philippine Development Plan, 1984-1987.

OLOFSON, Harold, ed. Adaptive Strategies and Change in the Philippine Swidden-Based Societies.

Peace Formation Program, Inc. On the Economic Crisis.

Philipine Business for Social Progress. Poverty Profile.

Philippine Peasant Institute. The National Peasant Situation: 1985.

POSTMA, Antoon. Mindanao Mangyan Mission.

Primer on the Rice Crisis.

REYNALDO, Hubert and Fern Babcock Gant, eds. The Isneg of the Northern Philippines: A Study of Trends of Change and Development.

RIVERA, Temerio C. "Capitalist Penetration into Agriculture: Some Issues on Land Concentration and Class Differentiation.

ROSENTHAL, Gerald. "Identifying the Poor: Economic Measure of Poverty".

SAJISE, Percy. Environmental Education and its Transfer: The Philippine Experience.

SCHIEGEL. Tiruray Justice.

SMITH, Ian, Miguel Ruzon and Carmen Vidal. Philippine Municipal Fisheries: A Review of Resources, Technology and Socio-Economics.

Social Forestry for Upland Development: Lessons for Four Case Studies.

TAN, E. A, and Y. Holazo. "Measuring Poverty Incidence in a Segmental Market: The Philippine Case".

Technological Board for Agricultural Credit. Socio-Economic Survey in Landless Rural Workers in Three Selected Barangays.

TOWNSEND, Peter. Poverty as Relative Deprivation: Resources and Style of Living.

131

United Nations Development Program/Food and Agriculture Organization. The Philippines, Shifting Cultivation, Demonstration and Training in Forest, Forest Range and Watershed Management.

United States Agency for International Development. Country Development Strategy Statement: FY 1982.

VALERIO, Teresita E., Aleta C. Domdom and Gracia M. Villavieja. An Analysis of Food Threshold in the Philippines.

WATTS, Harold W. The Iso-Prop Index: "An Approach to the Determination of Different Poverty Income Thresholds".

WEBB. "The Reaction of Native Proper to Resource Based on Economics".

World Bank. Aspects of Poverty in the Philippines: A Review and Assessment. World Bank Research Report. 1980.

Appendices

DEFINITIONS OF POVERTY

1. Charles Booth and Selbohm Rountru, two English Social Scientists, based their definition of poverty on the principle of minimum subsistence which, up to the present time, have been included in some form or the other in many poverty studies.

2. Jackson (1972) defined poverty as the failure to fulfill needs essential to social functioning. These needs were broadly categorized into stocks such as education, housing and security, and flows such as nutrition. Poverty is the result of failure of needs fulfillment. As this failure can occur in flows or in stocks, or both, poverty can be categorized into deprivation (the failure of stocks), and want (the failure of flows).

3. Peter Townsend (1975) defined poverty in terms of relative deprivation. Individuals, families and groups in the population can be said to be in poverty when they lack the resources to obtain the type of diets, participate in activities and have living conditions or "style of life" which are customary or at least widely encouraged or approved in the society in which they belong. The flow of resources are seriously below those commended by the average individual or family that they are, in effect, excluded from ordinary living patterns, customs and activities in their social areas.

4. Rosenthal (1968) considered identification of the poor as involving identifying those members of society whose consumption opportunity is low.

5. Watt's (1968) economic definition of poverty was based on a model of consumer choice. Poverty was defined as severe constriction of the choice set and measured by the consuming unit's generalized command over real goods and services.

6. The official definition of poverty of the United States Federal Government is based on a poverty line constructed

from the estimated income needed to purchase a nutritionally adequate diet on the assumption that one-third of the family income is spent on food.

7. The Ministry of Welfare Services in Malaysia identified a poverty line in connection with the ability of a family to remain in "good nutritional health" as well as to satisfy "minimum conventional needs in respect of clothing, household management, transport and communication." The minimum basket of food and non-food expenditures were then estimated to calculate the total poverty budget.

8. The United Nations (Organization) defined the poor as those living below what is considered the minimum level consistent with human dignity. Social well-being covers the basic necessities of food, clothing, shelter, education, health, etc. While what is basic or minimum in these items is a matter of definition, the size, age, levels, location of a family should be considered.

9. In terms of welfare, poverty is described by the U.S. Department of Health, Education and Welfare as insufficient income or other resources to provide the individual any or all of the necessities of life such as food, shelter, fuel, clothing and medical care for subsistence compatible with decency and health, with no persons legally liable and able to support him; or the total resources of an individual or family are insufficient to meet total requirements.

10. The United Nations Assistance to the Needy in Less-Developed Areas (LDA) described poverty in terms of welfare as the unavailability of the means of subsistence up to the level prevailing among the majority of the people living in the same town or community due to unemployment, physical and mental disability, old age or immaturity and other temporary or permanent circumstances.

11. In early Philippine studies, the term "low- income" was synonymous with "poor."

12. Another income-based concept used in the Philippines was the Rice-Wage Formula (RWF) of determining the poor, in-

troduced in 1946 by the Social Welfare Commission. The purchasing power (in terms of gantas of rice) that a family of a given size should have to be able to feed, clothe, shelter and educate the members decently was used to delineate the poverty threshold.

13. In the Philippines, many studies used poverty concepts based on minimum cost diets satisfying nutritional requirements recommended by the Food and Nutrition Research Institute (FNRI).

14. Valenzona (1976) used a poverty concept based on calorie requirements. She attempted to estimate the daily calorie requirements of a family according to its physical activity

15. Mangahas (1977) presented another definition of poverty based on perception concept. To arrive at a threshold, poverty is measured through the use of perception variables (e.g., perceived minimum needs in order that a family can consider itself non-poor).

16. The Ministry of Social Services and Development (MSSD) described poverty as the presence of grave financial need. Without definite sources of income or support either in cash or in kind, expenses for food, clothing, shelter and medical care could not be met by family income or other sources of livelihood.

17. The National Economic and Development Authority (NEDA) and the National Census and Statistics Office (NCSO) defined the low-income group as those households/families belonging to the bottom 30% of the income bracket which was also the basis of FNRI in doing a research study on low-income households in the Philippines. According to NEDA, the Philippines is using the bottom 30% as the definition of the low-income households. However, the definitions of low-income internationally is the group of households belonging to the bottom 40% of the income bracket.

The basic similarity among the concepts discussed is that the poor are those whose incomes barely maintain their physical existence and those who have limited or no means of access to other social needs.

137

PHILIPPINE
ENVIRONMENTAL PROFILE

The Philippines has a land area of 30 million hectares, distributed among 12 large and nine medium-sized islands, plus approximately 7,000 islets, reefs and atolls. The land-based eco-system is predominantly that of the tropical rain-forest. Approximately three million hectares have been converted over centuries to irrigated fields, and there are 120,000 hectares of grassland swamps. Eight hundred thousand (800,000) hectares are pine forest regions that are thought to be slowly evolving into more diverse tropical rainforest stands. Five million (5,000,000) hectares are *Imperata* type grasslands that were once forested. The principal tropical features of immense species diversity and a closed nutrient cycle which holds fertility mainly in the biomass are characteristic of the Philippines.

The coastline is 18,400 kms. long and has 400,000 hectares of mangrove eco-systems. Coral reefs on waters from 10-20 fathoms deep are estimated to cover a maximum of 33 million hectares.

With the exception of remote jungle areas and in seas bordering sparsely settled islands, all land, coastal and marine eco-systems have been altered, to a considerable degree, by human habitation or exploitation.

A rapidly expanding population plus random, uncontrolled physical growth of communities has been cited by the Philippine Government's National Environmental Protection Council (NEPC) as the principal cause of serious incompatibilities in land use patterns. Officially published reports of NEPC are summarized or quoted in this profile. These reports substantiate fears expressed by many observers that all of the various eco-system types found in the country are deteriorating.

Sustained economic, social and political stability are obviously related to the state of man's environment. Hence, the success or failure of development programs is necessarily affected by the degree to which development planning can effectively reconcile immediate human concerns with the dynamics of eco-systems developed over eons of evolution. These systems largely determine the extent and quality of all forms of life, whether measured over short, medium or long-term spans of time.

The principal Philippine environmental concerns are addressed below, as indicated by existing, although in many instances, incomplete research and official reports.

Soils

The deteriorating quality of soils is considered the most pressing environmental problem of the Philippines. Of the country's 11 million hectares of land developed principally to agriculture, three-fourths (75%) is badly eroded. On the balance of 19 million hectares, which are predominantly hilly or mountainous terrain, slash-and-burn farming, logging in excess of natural rates of regrowth, pasturing and fires have seriously depleted vegetative cover. The combination of sloping terrain, heavy tropical rains and insufficient vegetative cover has produced disastrous soil erosion. Five million hectares or one-sixth of the land area of the country is seriously denuded and degraded. Over one million hectares is considered to be in critical condition. Proper management and particularly fire protection would allow the natural dynamics of plant succession to function properly. Degraded lands can be rehabilitated through natural processes.

Forest

The extent of forest cover is uncertain. Satellite photograph interpreters have estimated that only about 20% of the total land area is covered by forests; government forest managers maintain the correct figure is 40%. Based on 1976 LANDSAT photographs, a Development Academy of the Philippines study indicates that 9,000,000 hectares or roughly 30% are adequately forested.

No matter which figure is correct, even the most optimistic estimates are far from encouraging. Forest cover is scattered sparsely over most of the Philippines. Relatively few locations contain most of the total forest cover, while many land areas are almost completely denuded. Serious floods and extensive siltation problems have been recurring annually, especially since 1970.

Commercial log extraction is governed by rules based on formulas adopted in the 1950's which sought to equate the rate of harvest with the rate of natural regrowth or regeneration. Concerned members of the research community have expressed the opinion that these official harvest rates far exceeded the rate of regrowth. Ressearch indicates that commercial logging may be removing timber three times faster than it can be replaced by new growth.

A far more serious problem is the clearing of rainforest for farming. Kaingeros precede or follow commercial loggers to slash-and-burn land for annual crops, principally rice and corn. This completely removes the vegetative cover when practiced on short rotations and causes a drastic change in biotic conditions. The removal of shade makes it virtually impossible for the original dipterocarp forest species to regenerate. These dominant species, and various associated plantfile, require shades in their early years of growth and will not tolerate exposure. As a result, grasses, particularly *Imperata cylindrina* and *Saccharum spontaneium*, quickly dominate the area. This is a significant step backwards in the evolutionary process. These grasses are almost invariably razed each dry season by man-made fires. This kills off other plant types that are struggling to establish themselves and effectively stops the natural succession process towards higher and more diverse plant populations from taking place. The grasses resprout from rhizomes and the process is repeated. Each burning depletes soil fertility, induces erosion and reduces the chances for successful reforestation, whether natural or artificially-induced.

Forests are also affected adversely by the fact that most of the population relies on firewood for cooking. It is estimated that at least 50% of wood cut down is used for firewood (UNDP).

Mangroves

There are approximately 400,000 hectares of mangrove eco-systems in the Philippines. Only five percent of Philippine mangroves are still in a virgin (i.e., undisturbed) state, while 45% are classified as young growth and 50% as reproduction brush.

One hundred seventy-five thousand (175,000) hectares have been converted into brackish water fishponds. Official estimates of mangrove areas still forested by *Rhizophora. Acicennia* and related species vary between 100,000 to 200,000 hectares.

Officially, the Philippine government has recognized the need to change emphasis from exploitation of mangroves to protection of this vital link in the nutrient cycle. The leasing of mangrove areas for conversion to new fishponds has been curtailed and emphasis placed instead on increasing yields from existing fishponds.

Mangroves are one of the most fertile and biologically productive eco-systems on the earth. Micronutrients produced in these systems are transported seaward, where phytoplankton photosynthesis takes place. Undisturbed mangroves are the nursery and feeding grounds of various forms of aquatic life, including many commercially important species of fish, shrimps, crabs and eels. Current research indicates the probability that production of food in marine areas may be greater if mangroves are undisturbed than if these tidelines are converted into ponds designed to induce production through artificial methods.

Coral Reefs

In terms of number and diversity of organisms, coral reefs are the richest eco-systems on earth. Approximately 400 of the 500 known species of corals are found in the Philippines and 15% of total marine fish production in the country is reportedly contributed by coral reefs.

The Philippine government research indicates that only five percent of the coral reefs are in excellent condition, 21% in good and 27% in fair condition. Nearly one-half (47%) are considered to be in poor condition. Philippine reefs are endangered by siltation, unregulated collection, destructive fishing methods, pollution and predation by the crown of thorns starfish *(Acanthaster planci)*.

Ninety (90) percent of traded corals are exported and an estimated 22,000 families are dependent on the coral industry. Dynamiting and, in some instances, trawl fishing cause serious and long-term damage to coral areas. Research data indicates that areas shattered by dynamite may take 40 years to reach 50% of their original growth.

Water Resources

Despite an average rainfall of 2,300 mm/year, three of the most densely populated regions (Central Luzon, Western Visayas and Central Visayas) may face critical water shortages within the next two decades. The Philippines has 421 principal rivers with drainage basis over 40 sq. km. each, 59 lakes covering 200,000 hectares, 130,000 hectares of artificial reservoirs and 126,000 hectares of freshwater swamps, pumping systems and municipal water supplies, with only minor attention paid to the need to improve or at least sustain acquifer recharge potential.

Research indicates that evapotranspiration recycles 2/3 of the rain falling on the land back into the atmosphere and that 23% of all runoff is accounted for in flood flows, most of which are unharnessed for human use. The natural hydrologic cycle moves water back onto the land, but accurate estimates of water supply have been inhibited by inconsistent and irregular collection of water data.

Immediate demands of a rapidly expanding population for more agricultural, industrial and municipal water supplies place tremendous pressure on government to invest available financial resources to try and satisfy these demands. This unfortunately limits the ability to take long-range measures required to store

142

water over large areas by the proper maintenance of natural acquifer recharge capacity. Soil erosion, deforestation and siltation have already reduced the expected life of many major investments in reservoirs for irrigation, hydro-electric power and domestic water supplies. Further, since most irrigation projects use diversion methods with small storage facilities, their efficiency is highly dependent on stream flow. The National Irrigation Administration estimates a loss of 35.5% of total irrigation potential during the dry season. The agricultural sector accounts for the largest percentage of total water demand, an estimated 83%.

Water quality is generally poor in the rural areas with high levels of bacterial contamination. Pollution from pesticides and chemical fertilizers is increasing. In urban centers where approximately 35% of the population resides, human waste and garbage are polluting many sources of surface and groundwater. This is particularly true in the Metro Manila area where 15% of the population and most industries are concentrated. Sixty percent of the pollution load is attributed to inadequate sewerage and garbage disposal systems. Industry accounts for 40% of water pollution. Laguna de Bay, the nation's largest lake, located within the Metro Manila area, is in a severely eutrophic state principally because of human and domestic wastes, although agricultural run-off is considered significant and industrial pollution is increasing.

Fisheries

Approximately 60% of total marine catch is harvested in shallow coastal waters by an estimated 560,000 artisanal fishermen who practice this trade part-time or full-time. The coastal waters are considered to be fully exploited. Deep sea fishing is on the increase and may eventually supply more of the national food requirements. However, the continued increase in the cost of fuel might affect this trend.

NEPC reports that illegal fishing practices throughout the Philippines are perhaps the greatest current threats to aquatic resources. Fine meshed nets, dynamite, poisons and electrical devices, as well as commercial trawl fishing in waters less than seven fathoms deep, are identified as the principal danger. Destruction of mangrove eco-systems can also contribute to depletion of fishery resources since the mangroves are a vital link in the food chain supporting marine life.

There are indications of over-exploitation in several areas, namely, Manila Bay, San Miguel Bay, the Pacific side of Bohol and the Samar sea. Declining yields have been recorded. On the other hand, deep sea waters are considered under-exploited. Philippine territorial waters cover approximately 1,660,000 sq.km., coastal waters are only 265,973 sq. km. of this total.

Inland fisheries production is expected to increase but these sites are sensitive to the dangers posed by siltation and water pollution.

Air Quality, Noise, Housing, Environmental Health and Sanitation

These closely inter-related issues generally affect the large centers of population, as increasing numbers of rural people migrate to the cities.

Numerous papers have been published on the problems inherent to situations wherein a majority of urban dwellers live as squatters in slum areas. The Philippines is no exception in this regard and the environmental dangers of such a situation are well recognized.

Research by NEPC indicates that a rapidly expanding population and uncontrolled physical growth of communities are the principal causes of serious incompatibilities in land use patterns. Most of the population is poor and has to survive from day-to-day, often at the expense of the environment.

Conclusion

The "pollution of poverty" is, in the final analysis, the principal factor affecting Philippine environmental conditions. Natural resource exploitation for immediate economic returns is difficult to reconcile with long-term environmental considerations.

144

Land uses that result in soil erosion and forest destruction are difficult to alter when immediate concerns make tremendous demands on scant resources. And yet an overview of Philippine environmental issues indicates that these two basic concerns are the major threats to water supplies and quality, coastal eco-systems, wildlife populations and most other environmental quality indicators.

These resources are, and probably will continue to be, the basic source of livelihood of most of the population in the foreseeable future. There is a limit to the amount of stress these resources can withstand. Once the point of irreversible environmental decline is reached, any progress in development attained in the interim will be gradually, but inexorably, lost. This may already be taking place. The first victims will be the poorer elements of society as their traditional income sources disappear.

(Source: United States Agency for International Development)